The Only Way Out

Jess Knutson

Copyright © 2021 Jess Knutson

All rights reserved.

ISBN: 978-1-7373111-0-2

DEDICATION

This book is dedicated to anyone who just needs to hear that eventually, shit does get better.

For the daydreamers.

The goal chasers.

TABLE OF CONTENTS

Holy Shit... I Did It	6
Pregame Pep Talk	9
On Guard	13
Losing Myself	17
Hey Alexa... What's Another Word For Growth?	25
Heroes	28
So... This is Forever	34
Jess is Sus...	44
See You Later	48
The Actual Most Important Never Ending Chapter	56
Truth or Likes?	60
Intuition	64
A Dark Night	70
Do What Works	80
Scars	82
Reflections	86
Kindling	92
An Equal But Opposite Reaction	95

Prioritize You	98
Love	103
Just For Now	107
Slow	109
Pride	115
Reflection	118
Coexist	123
Thanks For The Memories	126

Holy Shit... I Did It

If you're holding this book in your incredible hands, it means I actually did it. I started writing this book after having it be my brain baby for several years. Do you know what stopped me for all this time?

Fear.

Fear of being vulnerable,
fear of people 'knowing' me,
fear of failure,
fear of how these stories might change how some people view me,
fear of doing something that I didn't even know how I would ever accomplish.
Fear of visiting with my past and putting it all out there for the world to ingest.
Fear of fallout.
Fear of what was to come.

I could (and did) come up with hundreds of reasons why I shouldn't make this dream a reality. Yet there was always this one teenage nagging voice in the back of my head giving me one reason why I should, and do you know what that reason was? Because I wanted to. No matter how loud the thoughts were that told me I shouldn't, it was that one little consistent voice that one day I chose to listen to. My own. If I hadn't, that would mean closing a door on a dream of mine.

I finally just had to decide that the risk of failure was worth it. I needed to find a way to channel these thoughts, feelings and experiences in a healthy manner. This way, I can help other people that may someday find themselves in shoes similar to mine. If I can prevent some of these things from happening at all, for anyone; If I could make that happen even just once, then I couldn't actually fail. And so, the journey began.

On top of the emotional piece (as if that wasn't enough of an avoidant already) there is so much pressure to achieve perfection in today's digitally skewed variant of reality. I'm making it my personal mission to show people that imperfection is awesome. Not only is imperfection awesome, it's so common! It's also totally and completely relevant to pretty much everything. Doing things that may not make sense to other people is actually what life is all about. Finding your true authentic self. This version of you is so much more fun and rewarding than trying to fit the impossible mold that society deems we should fit into.

SPOILER ALERT: people like that actually don't exist.

You don't, I don't, even your grandmother doesn't - although if she's anything like my grandmothers... she is likely to be the closest to the human embodiment of literal perfection as we know it.

In preparation for this creation, I scoured the internet for book reviews online to thicken my skin and to see if I can determine what people usually find as the most disappointing thing when they're looking forward to reading a book. While I am a bit biased, I am attempting to compile a list of things this book does have... because the list of what it doesn't have is much, much longer. Some of the content you'll find hidden in these pages that are not for everyone include:

- Sarcasm

- Swearing
- Physical, emotional, and mental abuse
- Sketchy grammar
- Astrology & horoscope references
- Mentions of bodily functions
- Last but not least, you'll bear witness to some of my very own imperfect decision making skills.

Now I feel as though I have fully prepared any reader for the general feel of this fine work of literature and they can now set their standards to a more reasonable level. Seriously though, if you hate a book - don't spend the precious moments of your life finishing it. I would be more offended knowing you finished this book and hated it rather than spending time doing things you love. If any of the aforementioned bullets anger, trigger or frustrate you or you don't like laughing and having fun, I am not for you and this book is probably better off being donated somewhere. In fact, bring it to someone you hate.

I am so sorry if you received this book as a gift.

In all seriousness though, thank you for picking up this collection of stories, life lessons, essays... however you want to identify it. It's people like you who help make people's dreams come true. I feel so incredibly honored to share this space with you. Thank you, from the bottom of my heart.

Pregame Pep Talk

I do not claim to be highly educated in the subject of proper grammar and all writing techniques. My reality is that I am someone who has always enjoyed reading and writing. I have lived part of a life, and I want to share my weak points with you in a move of solidarity through this journey thus far. If this relieves some of the anxiety you have in your life around how different your life looks compared to friends on social media, then my job here is done.

I am HERE for you.

I will be one of the authentic few to show you just how messy a life can be. My take is that experience is life's greatest teacher. We are going to pair life lessons with vulnerability. Our experiences are valid and worthy without having to pay an institution $50,000 for a piece of paper proving otherwise.

My experiences paired with my incredible story telling abilities have allowed me to bless this universe with this literary gold. I want to prove that you absolutely can have big goals and aspirations. You can have these goals for yourself and even accomplish them. You don't have to feel guilty, you don't have to feel bad about claiming your time as your own.

I knew from the jump that publishing this book would be hella hard. Getting all of these stories and emotions out on the table, navigating conversations around a process that I am 100% clueless about. However, my longing to reach out to other people who feel as though they ride the struggle bus and hardly make it through the day is bigger than just holding everything in and dare I say, feeling the shame that comes along with it. More often than not at this point in life days are hard. Which is exactly why I'm writing this book. You are not alone in your insecurity. I made a goal of reaching out to others, in a way that felt safe and relatable, yet not all encompassing and still private. I will forever be an advocate of flexibility and doing things your own way and on your own terms. If I can convey these thoughts and feelings and connect with people during an act of self care for the both of us, it helps us as a collective feel less alone.

Most of all I want to prove to people that even when life feels chaotic, you can still achieve goals that make *you* happy. Create goals for yourself, give yourself some grace and goodness gracious LOVE YOURSELF SOME MORE. Life is hard enough as it is. Make sure you're not making it more difficult for yourself when you don't even have to. We need to get rid of this notion that people are only as valuable as their productivity. Because that's bullshit. We as humans actually don't (and shouldn't) have to come last. I hope that you feel that, genuinely in your heart by the end of this book. We don't have to be perfect to be valued. We don't have to be selfless anymore. We are allowed to be humans too. Our hopes and dreams are just as valid as those we idolize. We can have goals and mindfully use our time to complete these things even in the rudimentary lens we view our life. We grow the most in those uncomfortable, vulnerable moments.

I wrote a book because quite honestly I care. I care enough about my goals and aspirations and I care about your goals and aspirations. Even if you don't quite know what they are yet. We don't need to live aesthetically pleasing lives and broadcast them for the world to see for our work to be meaningful or to get something out of it. I am living proof that you can be a mom with a chronic illness, a difficult past, anxiety, and still find time to write a book. Sure, it might take a little longer than someone else who maybe lives in NY and doesn't have children and a chronic illness and probably has a beautiful view of the city and makes a million dollars a second... but at the end of the day - even though our situations are vastly different, at the heart of it all, our goal is the same. Our paths will be different.

Even though the route to our destinations differ, our processes are still meaningful. We are still growing, learning and doing something we love. In turn, taking care of ourselves. I want to make sure you are taking care of you, whether that means just taking time to curl up with a good book *ahem* (thank you), daydreaming about your goals, becoming an artist, learning hip hop dances, reading a hundred books, learning a skill, whatever the case may be. I want to make sure you're living your life for you and finding things you enjoy. I want to inspire you to participate in those activities more often, do something that fills your soul up because you are more than your production. People don't take the time to tap into that part of themselves anymore, and it shows up loud in the world we live in.

I know it's hard to have goals. I know it. I can't say I blame people for not having personal ambition because within the society we live in currently, how can you not be exhausted and burned out by 2:00 everyday? News Flash! It's not a 2:00 slump, people, it's because we're doing way too much every day and by 2:00 our bodies are ready to be done and start winding down because of the amount of stress we're constantly experiencing.

But alas, there is always work to do so fuel yourself up with caffeine and let capitalism wring the last few hours of productivity they can get from you before you're on your way home, knowing damn well once you sit down on the couch you're not getting back up until it's time for bed.

Our lives are more than that. We, as people, are more than that. Let's find our fires and passions. Let's create time to participate in activities that set our souls on fire. I hope you will make your time available to yourself, because you're worth it.

Start as small or slow as you need to.

Ink yourself into your own schedule.

On Guard

The other day my daughter and I were driving home from a place I cannot remember. We turned onto a street not too far from our house. It's one of my favorite winding roads, actually. This road turns into something incredibly special in the fall because the streets are lined with trees that canopy over the top of the road. Pair that little cocoon with the colors of fall in Minnesota. The view is truly magnificent.

My daughter has always loved her one on one time. Truth be told, I love it too. She has so much to say and I love to listen to her emptying her brain. Her world view and visions of improving life as we know it give me so much hope for the future. We have the same sense of humor. She's overall a great conversationalist.

She also knows how to read people and their energies. She can find out what you love, and what makes you tick without ever asking you a question. She loves to learn with fun, silly questions, and then throw a really deep one in the mix to throw you off her tracks. That's exactly what she did to me on this very day. On this very drive home. It was not the first time, and I know deep in my soul it won't be the last. We were laughing, acting out a fake, funny scenario in a storyline format into the air in front of us. There were deep belly laughs, further additions to the story, followed by more laughs, followed by more scenario... and you catch my drift. We were straight up having a good time.

"Mom..." there was a lingering pause. I knew what was coming, it was one of her infamous bombshell questions "What's the most traumatic thing that's ever happened to you?"

I lost my breath at that moment.

She's a wonderer. Her imagination takes her places most of us have never dreamed. She has an instinct that is so strong she routinely knows things before she even asks the questions. Her mind never stops. It has been a goal of mine to teach my children that they are multifaceted human beings. Not only are *they* multifaceted, but so am I. I can be so many different things than just mom. A lesson I hope that they carry with them into the future should they choose to become parents themselves. You don't need to change who you are based on your title.

Instinctively, I jolted my head to look at her and I asked her, "What?"

This was not because I didn't hear her, but because I needed some time to further digest the question that was currently just hovering like a cloud of smoke in the air between us. She repeated herself. "What's the most traumatic thing that has ever happened to you?" aware of the impact her question had on me. I had mere seconds to decide how to respond to this question. My decision was to respond honestly.

I know this can be uncomfortable for some people, especially with their children. We want them to believe that this life treats you well and negative events and their corresponding perceived negative emotions are few and far between, but truth be told they are just not. We need to be honest about that. Don't cripple your children's coping skills from the jump because we're hiding how stressful and heartbreaking and unnerving the world can be. Don't do them that disservice. If you were never taught to cope with hard things, learn. Teach them. Learn together. Communicate your feelings.

Honesty in this situation looked like this. "It was something that happened a long time ago, but right now it's not something I'm ready to talk about."

Of course, this only piqued her curiosity. If she wasn't going to find out what happened directly, she wanted to know when it happened, where, who I was with and let me tell you - for a person with PTSD this was a tough conversation to hold it together. She was spewing questions at me and each one feeling like a stab to the psyche. I know she didn't realize what was going on with me internally. She was asking out of her deep care for me.

I have been in situations where I feared that I had lived out my final day, breathing my final breaths. So naturally, my first reaction in this situation was to get defensive. I wanted to tell her that it wasn't an appropriate story to talk to my 9 year old about right now, and that I didn't want to talk about this traumatic situation. However, I know that her intention was to connect with me. We were having fun and being open, we were connecting on her level. I assured her that someday it would be a story I would share with her but that day would not be today. It's an event that I still need to process on my own.

I reminded her that I love our time together and I hope that she never gets tired of asking questions. I also slightly suggested that maybe we should refrain from just asking people questions like that randomly because it can bring up some negative emotions and be traumatic for some people. She understood, and we moved on with our day.

Parenthood always has me on guard. Whether it's me being on guard for my children around other people, or me being on guard for these bombshell questions that happen in the middle of everyday life when you least expect it. We only learn how to cope with these situations by being put in them. The universe and this life works in mysterious ways.

Pain is part of the process.
Pain is necessary to give the alternative meaning.

Keep your guard up, but remember that there is also profound beauty and potential in each vulnerability.

Losing Myself

To be completely honest with you, I hadn't even started remotely understanding myself until I was 32 years old. I went to a very small town high school back when it was more of a rural area. To set the scene, I'm feeling compelled to tell you about a small town rumor I heard once upon a time. Across the street from my high school used to be a plot of farm land. The farmer who owned the property was upset about someone asking him about his fertilizing plan that he then (passive aggressively, like any true Minnesotan) would pile manure up near the busiest intersection in town, every summer. It never failed that on the hottest days the town always smelled atrocious. Just a hot, heaping pile of steaming shit. I remember stopping at what used to be an intersection, always feeling so bad for the houses located near that particular field. Those people who lived there probably couldn't even open their windows on nice days because their whole environment would smell like hot shit.

Even though in the beginning, we migrated from one small town to another, I never felt that I really 'fit in' anywhere with the vast majority of the people on my second go round. I went from having close friends, participating in sports and having foundational relationships, to moving to a completely new place where I didn't know a soul. I no longer had a social life nor participated in activities like I did in my previous life. I felt as though I lost everything I held dear to me. I moved at the beginning of junior high, 7th grade - everyone in this school already had their established group of friends by this point and there were no more "spots at the lunch table" literally and figuratively, for newbies. I lost my whole life.

A lot of these well established friend groups doubled as cousins and other distant relatives. Needless to say, these people were together all the time. The term 'clique' didn't even describe just how shut out new people were in this environment.

I don't really know if all of them were aware of how unwelcoming they were to new people, but a select few of them made it known that they were aware, and didn't give a shit about your existence or where you came from. Unless they could, of course, use you for something or make you a target of their own jokes. There's a saying that kids are cruel. I don't buy that. Kids can be cruel. Being cruel is a learned behavior or perhaps a mental illness and needs to be addressed as such. Just saying 'kids are assholes' and not doing anything about it makes you part of the problem.

Eventually, there were enough of us newbies to draw some attention and bring some of the townies out to play... the version of these people that I knew were nice enough people. I don't know how life has chewed them up and spit them out to tell you if that's still the case. However, once high school was over I lost touch with nearly all of those people. Maybe they're nice people now, but that doesn't negate the fact that some of their behaviors contributed to a very isolating time in what was no doubt an imperative era for meaningful connections in my own life.

I am confident this is where my journey into introversion started, or was unearthed. I carried the weight of my emotions from my parents divorce, the uproot of my entire life as I knew it, and my incredible loneliness. This is where I took my hurt, pain, and grief and bottled it all up. I hoarded all these little bottles of sorrow and unspoken outrage and uncried tears and bleeding proverbial emotional wounds. Eventually I had so many bottles of darkness that I was disassociating myself from any actual emotion. I was a prisoner to whatever bottle fell off the shelf and hit me in the head that day, and I suffered in utter silence with all of these emotions for years. Day after day after day.

I met my current best friend the year of 8th grade, and even for a while we had an unspoken understanding that we were in this whole high school thing together, but we also just kind of existed parallel to one another until we were sure that each of us as newbies vibrated on the same level. We bonded over our loneliness and the shittiness of the new town our parents made us live in. My best memories from high school include her - we were a beacon of light atop a lighthouse for each other. To this day, that light continues to shine regardless of how many miles or minutes or time between phone calls betwixt one another. She is my person and she will forever be my person. I love you.

Not much time had passed after high school ended and I exited that red and brown brick building into the manure tinged air to face this world head on. However the universe had other plans to aggressively hurl me right into the terrible abyss of adulthood. It was only three short months after my high school graduation I found out I was pregnant. At my first OB appointment, the best little Finnish doctor swirled her little period tracking chart and announced, "June 4th, 2007... that is your due date."

Exactly one year from my high school graduation and just look at me, a baby getting ready to have a baby and I didn't even realize it. I had no idea how my story was about to pivot.

There's this thing that happens when you're a teenager and you have a baby. As fast as a baby can exit your body, all of a sudden your friends just seemingly, disappear. The 'let me know when you need a baby sitter!" turns into texts left on read (which wasn't actually a thing then but, you get what I'm saying) and your calls being forwarded to voicemail. Your contacts seem to back away from you slowly, arms reached outwards. Teens just don't want to hang around a baby. I get it. Being a newly adult teen and caring for infants are very paradoxical stages of life. But again, as I was used to doing, I pulled back and wrapped myself in a blanket of depression on top of my hoard of hurt. This turned out to be a dangerous combination for me as a whole.

The very truth of it is, it was astonishingly alienating. All my fellow former teen moms out there FEEL me on this. This was a whole new level of loneliness. There I was, yet again in some very definitive years of establishing my identity and I spent it mostly alone; taking care of an infant, working full time, trying to further my education, pay my rent, and prove to myself I was worthy of being loved by another human. I was wrapping my arms around understanding I was in no way even remotely close to being an adult.

But wait!
There's more!

I was involved in an abusive relationship on all levels. Not to mention in the midst of it all, I was trying to get answers to what I would later come to understand is a chronic, life interrupting painful health ailments.

I can confirm this is not the best environment to try and understand what you weren't taught in school while trying to define who you are and what you want out of life all while shaping another little human from the depths of sleep deprivation.

Needless to say, my mental health spiraled out of control; unraveling at speeds I couldn't comprehend. I didn't have the time, nor did I even realize I was not taking care of myself. This showed in the vast majority of choices that followed over the course of the next several years. Each and every day the goal was to quite literally just make it through the day. I would spend my time daydreaming about the moment that I could lay back down and close my eyes to escape to an unconscious state and avoid the reality and the pain that existed within my being. If I could do just that, the day was a success. Minimal thinking - mainly surviving, but only just barely. My person had switched to autopilot. I was not prepared for any of this.

I was rolling through the motions of my days, I wasn't critically thinking and just existing in survival mode. Survival mode for me meant It became habitual that every decision I made was only decided after taking into account how it affected everyone else - even if a particular solution made things worse for me. This habit continued until my thirties, yall... far, far too long.

I was made to believe that I was only as valuable as my self sacrifice. That's one of the fascinating things about doing this inner work is looking back and reflecting on who you are and why you do the things you do. So many things become crystal quartz clear during the process.

Near my low point in life I made decisions based on other people's wants, needs and reactions. This framework molded itself into one of my most used decision making processes for over a decade. That's far too long of saying 'no' to myself. It's a long time to let myself down and sacrifice my own needs, wants and desires for others.

And for what? No one was rearranging their life to reciprocate the effort I was making.

To do something like this out of habit is just, kind of sad, isn't it? The thing about this autopilot mode is sometimes it's an incredibly hard switch to turn off, especially if it's been in the 'on' position for an extended period of time. It was a familiar process. The more I denied myself, the easier it became to do it consistently.

As humans our brains like patterns and our brain likes what's known and what's comfortable. Change can be hard and in some cases, change can be terrifying. Going against the easy and comfortable choice means choosing the road less traveled. Choosing the path of more resistance goes against what you know, but the more you do it, the stronger your brain becomes at making choices based on you. It's all about having a growth mindset. Life becomes a million times more fascinating when you're able to make connections and watch yourself grow.

Take it from me, I know that getting to know yourself is hard. Knowing where to start is hard. At times you'll catch yourself avoiding it. During the process you'll get to see the golden, sparkly, beautiful parts of yourself, and the dark, shadowy parts filled to the rim with grief and heartache. You get to drill down to find out what blocks and bricks make you who you are. You'll discover the material of your foundation; where you choose to let the light in, and choose which shadows you elect to bring to light. You have the choice and the option to heal from things that hurt you. You can put the baggage down where it lies and walk away. Sometimes you'll need to organize what thoughts actually belong to you, and what doesn't in an effort to lighten your load. You don't have to carry it all. Put it down.

Life is a whole ass journey with an unknown departure date and trust me when I say it's in your best interest to fill your luggage of this life journey with joy and beautiful memories instead of letting the darkness own your space and filling your suitcases to the brim with things that are no longer serving (or have ever served) your best interest.

When I first started wanting to take a closer look at my life, I didn't know how I was going to go about doing such a thing when I couldn't remember a lot of my past. One wild symptom about living in survival mode is the memory loss that comes with it. You're so zoned in on survival and just making it through each day, disassociated. It's like your memory just doesn't have the capacity to file these memories away. Your thoughts are consumed with planning out conversations you need to have in your head in an effort to make sure what you say can't be misconstrued into making someone upset or inconvenienced. It's diluting your emotions and feelings to make others comfortable and content. All the while feeling like you're dying inside. It's wanting to just cease to exist because you feel like your only purpose is to serve everyone except yourself.

When I first started doing this inner discovery work, I could recall general timelines, or memories would bubble up to the surface if someone starts talking about them in depth - but had someone else not brought it up first, it'd be nothing I could have remembered on my own. Sometimes it freaks me out a little bit how much I spaced out on just trying to survive. That was worth it in the end because had I been trying to process active trauma I don't know that I would have been able to withstand that phase of my life.

At the end of the day, we've all had our low points and felt like we've hit the absolute bottom. If you haven't, wow, congratulations and I am very happy that happened for you. Please know that if you have hit the bottom (like myself and many, many, countless others) I felt like I was making the best decisions with the reasonings and the life experience that I had at the time. I now know I can't dwell on those past experiences too much in a negative way. I only look back to see how far I've come. And maybe apologize to myself for letting things go the way I did. My perspective on these situations look a lot different these days, and if that's not growth I don't know what is.

After all, they have taught me so much in retrospect. I have a beautiful family, my children and I survived the time and they are some of the most incredible humans I know. So, things have turned out alright so far. I didn't have to force my husband to marry me, and we have perfect friends. So, even though it's possible to lose yourself. You can be cognizant of who you are at below rock bottom, you can rebuild with a deep, solid foundation and have the life you always dreamed of having. You can do this on your own schedule, and complete these goals in whatever order you want. Life doesn't have to be perfect or done on a societal timeline to be absolutely breathtaking.

It's possible.

It is so, so possible.

"Hey Alexa... What's another word for growth?"

Does Alexa even do that? I don't know. We had an Alexa plugged in our house for about six minutes before one of my children took the charger for one of their gadgets and we've never heard from her again. She just sits unused, behind the Roku player collecting dust and doing whatever else she can do without a functioning power source.

I have to say, growth is a high school bitch of a process. One minute you feel good as fuck, prancing around in your underwear and robe singing into a psuedo microphone - hair in a towel and feeling good as hell. You're doing all the self care feeling like the shiniest of stars, radiating abundance and sheer joy everywhere you go. Then, the next moment you're hit with a heaping pile of grief, sadness, or just overall flaming shitpile also known as growth. You'll feel like you're laying in a ditch, covered in mud - just praying to some higher power to be put out of your misery. That's growth.

A lot of people see the gleaming, beautiful side of growth, and think they want to do the work. They want to do that; live their most authentic life at 100 proof. They want to be someone who is finding beauty everywhere they go and be one of the people who have a smile that you can just tell radiates from deep within; the soul smile.

The side we fail to see and often publicize is the side of the process where you're buried, bursting out of your shell in the dark, cold, lonely space. The part where you're alone with your thoughts. The parts where you're analyzing everything you've ever known and you feel the most alone you've ever felt. During this process, emotional new truths and thought processes begin to grow. Your intuition develops. You will bust your new self out of old barriers.

The not pleasant piece can be too much for some people, so they never do it. They prefer to stay tucked and warm in their own little pod. They sit with the comfortable, the easy, the known. They regurgitate things that they've been conditioned to think and are not interested in sitting with the rejection, admittance of fear and shortcomings - this is all far too much of a burden to bear than facing the shame of potential rejection and failure. Getting to know yourself is too scary - outgrowing relationships feels harrowing and you're led to a headspace that you've never known. It's isolating, and you need to learn to exist as this version of yourself. This is when it's important to be your own biggest cheerleader, to participate in self care, and have an invaluable support system.

I can tell you one thing, though. When you get to those bright moments, sashaying your way through life, sharing big belly laughs and relishing in the moments you can appreciate your growth, it truly does make all the shitty parts of the expansion piece all worth it. You'll start seeing life with a new clarity and the character of your thoughts shift. Temporary shit for more intense happiness and radical self acceptance? I'll take it.

I was thinking recently about how different of a person I am now than I was at just the beginning of this year. The comparisons continued as I carried on to place these versions of me in juxtaposition to one another - the year prior, and three years. It truly is mind blowing how much has changed and how far I have come. All of the changes in my thinking and my worldview have culminated into who I am now, but I am not yet where I am going to be and damn, that's so compelling. I am seeking out to know more, see more, experience more - because that's what I need to be the best rendition of myself in each moment.

I don't want to give too much away, because honestly even though it's taken me a long time to come around to liking myself, I'm getting there. Trust me when I say there is still more room for work to be done, and I hope there is always room for me to find more room for joy and beauty and presence and learning in my days. I wouldn't be who I am without going through each and every one of these experiences, but if I can save someone else even a touch of heartache on this journey of life, then I'll do just that. I can't save you from all of it, though, because in this life we are all just a product of our experiences and all of our experiences are not bound to be positive. You are no exception.

If there was one thing I could tell my younger self, I would tell her that you handle this life with grace, by doing your best, holding your head up, and sending shooting star middle fingers to what everyone else thinks. You get there. You aren't a statistic. You don't come last. You make it.

And I remind her of that nearly every day.

Heroes

I quite literally have the best family in the world.

My grandmother married at 18 years old. Never worked a day in her life until after my grandfather passed away. His earthly departure left her with 5 kids to finish raising fully on her own. She did it, and she did a damn good job. I cannot fathom losing my husband one agonizing day and immediately my life flips upside down. Suddenly becoming the sole caregiver of everyone. Raising a family back then, trying to grieve your husband and raise your grieving children and get dinner on the table, feed the dog, and get to work on time... she later remarried and lost her second husband. She has since lived through the trauma of losing two of her own children, and outliving her siblings. For a woman who has endured so much, we can always count on Grammy to bring a smile to our faces with her animated storytelling abilities that I inherited with absolute pride. We can feel her love wrapping us in one of her quilts she's made for quite literally everyone she knows. She buzzes around town visiting friends and having lunches. She'll babysit her great grandkids and even travel three hours to do it! She's an incredible woman. I've admired her since the day I was born, and I'll admire her until the day I take my last breath. Likely even after that if I'm being honest. Eternal spirit adoration, it'll be my new thing.

My mother. Most everything she does comes from her heart. She cares about people. She raised my sister and I even though there were times I knew life wasn't easy for her. Losing her father at a young age was ruthless on her heart. Raising two kids alone is hard for anyone, and she handled it with grace and by providing stability. There were times I know that she doubted herself, or the job she was doing with my sister and I. To this day she thinks about things and wishes she would have done certain things differently. It's so easy to be hard on yourself as a parent. My mother does an incredible job. My sister and I never missed a meal, we had a roof over our heads, clothes to wear, friends to meet up with, cars to drive, phones to connect with people, money to go out and do things. We have a mom who loves us dearly. Who cared enough to try and take an interest in our lives and to teach us how to be responsible. My mom has taught me resourcefulness, stubbornness, and how to never rely on someone else to do something for you. Some would argue this is annoying, but I quite enjoy it sometimes. She's funny, she's smart, and it's always a compliment to me when people say that my mom, my sister and I are very alike in our mannerisms. It makes sense. Yet another badge of honor.

Uncle Rick. I don't think there are enough words that I could string along in the english language for me to actually accurately depict Uncle Rick as a person. He genuinely was one of the greatest people to ever exist. He loved his friends, his family, and his motorcycle. He couldn't stand Hollywood and thought everything was ridiculously funny. Listening to his reasoning and telling us his thoughts always ended with me in tears because he was just so damn funny. He was the type of dude you could never actually get through a TV show with - let alone a movie because the man would never shut up about how fake everything was, or how this thing or that thing couldn't actually physically happen or how this actor said something stupid this one time or how they wore a stupid shirt once. As he got older, he missed how life 'used to be'. He had a love for his dogs that was unmatched. He never missed a chance to take his motorcycle out for a spin. He visited his friends often. One this is for sure, one of his favorite activities was going up into the hills for a little 'fresh air'. He always came back down that hill as the best version of himself.

Uncle Rick was born with a genetic disorder called Gardner's Syndrome. Gardner's Syndrome causes tumors to grow, both cancerous and non cancerous and is linked to early age colon cancer.
Despite this diagnosis, Uncle Rick lived a pretty full life. He lived with his brother Ed, who also had Gardner's Syndrome, until Ed met his wife Patty and he moved to Missori to start their lives together. Rick served in the United States Army, enjoyed fishing, spending time with his best friend Roger. He would do a lot of traveling from his house to the Mayo Clinic in Rochester, Minnesota to attend doctor appointments. For as long as I had known him, he had never been in a relationship, and had never had any kids. As a child I asked him about this, and he told me that my cousins and I were enough fun for him, and that we were all he needed. I asked my mom about this a few years later and she told me that he never got involved with anyone or had kids because he didn't want to take the chance of spreading Gardner's to anyone else. He was the most selfless man I have ever met. His goal was to stop the spread of a genetic disorder that had been running rampant on one side of my family for generations, and to me that is just such a humanitarian thing to do. I will forever honor him for the many sacrifices he made on behalf of his own self.

It's a strange thing to say, but Uncle Rick and I had always bonded over our digestive issues. Me having Crohn's, he was very familiar with a lot of the procedures I had to have and a lot of the medications I had to take. He would tell me a lot about his procedures and he would always remind me how important it was that I was taking care of myself. He would ask about my doctors and encouraged me to switch if I didn't like them. He gave me tips on what to say or ask certain questions.. Kind of like, tricks of the trade, if you will. He was not okay with me putting myself second and he wanted to make sure that I wasn't doing anything that was going to put me at any kind of risk. A lot of it had to do with the fact that he knew my pain, and he absolutely hated that I was going through it. I could tell by the look in his eyes when he'd talk to me and when he'd get his serious voice on when he told me to make sure I kept going to see my doctor.

His last days here on earth were some of the hardest I have ever experienced. I had never been in such close proximity to death with someone I had known my whole life, and wow... that was a lot.

When someone passes away I think a lot of people think that if they could have seen their loved one 'one last time' they would have said 'this' or done 'that'. I am here to tell you that even when you know it's the last time... it's still the hardest. It took me two hours to leave that day. Going back and forth pacing the front door and the hospital bed my uncle laid in. I paced around the room because I didn't know what I wanted the last thing I would to say to him to be. Part of me knew that it'd be the last time and that alone was reason enough for me to never want to leave. Deep down I knew he wouldn't want me to be present when he ascended into his next journey.

Sure enough, about 12 hours after I got home, and after my cousins and my sister had left, he made his earthly departure. I'll never forget that day.

I was at Menards, picking out a rug. Naturally my reaction after returning home was that I immediately needed to redecorate my living room because grief is weird.

I was standing in the aisle, looking through rugs like you used to flip through the poster display at Walmart. I felt a buzz in my hoodie pocket and pulled out my phone. A picture of my mom, and bold white text that said "Momma" flashed across the screen and I already knew. Before I even picked up the call, I knew exactly what she was going to tell me. I slid my shaky finger across the 'slide to answer' dial on my screen. All I heard was a gasp.

Believe it or not suddenly my choice in rugs didn't seem so vital as it did just thirty seconds ago. My heart shattered into pieces on the concrete floor as I heard my mom say, 'he's gone' through gasps of her own grief of losing another one of her big brothers. When I hung up, I got some weird stares, but it didn't matter. At that very moment in time, nothing mattered. My husband held me in the middle of the flooring aisle, he tried to catch me piece by piece as I fell apart inside of the home improvement warehouse. I still have only been down that aisle one other time since - and I still am not in love with the rug I chose that day.

Uncle Rick will forever be held in high regard in my book. He lived his life basking in laughter, fun, fresh air, and love. He was grounded. He loved his family, his nieces and nephews, his dogs, his parents, his siblings, and making people laugh. He loved fishing, riding his motorcycle, riling up his great nieces and great nephews, talking shit, Harley's and cheesy potatoes at thanksgiving time. I think about him every time I pass a motorcycle on the road, or hear any AC/DC songs. He will forever hold a special place in my heart, and he will forever be my hero.

He told me once that he never set out to be someone's hero, that he was far from perfect. He just wanted to be a good person.

That's what makes him the best kind of hero to me.

So... This is Forever

I started having stomach problems at 16 years old. At many subsequent doctor visits I was diagnosed with everything from gastritis to heartburn. Around the age of 18, my stomach issues started getting worse. I spent years in and out of urgent care and the emergency room. It was probably the most expensive time period in my life because like a true rebel (or maybe child who didn't know anything) I was just out and about in the world without health insurance. I was fresh out of high school and my high school paying job didn't exactly leave me enough to enroll into any insurance plan. While most of my peers were going to college and traveling and buying homes. I was getting bills in the mail that ballooned from $250 a visit all the way up to $47,000 for some visits. I was the proud owner of not just one, or two, or three of those bills. In fact, I can't even tell you how many of those bills I racked up over the course of the six years it took me to get an actual diagnosis of what was truly causing all of my issues.

Six years.

But alas, each time I was told that because I wasn't seemingly dying at that very moment there was nothing that the great american health system could do for me. It was suggested time and time again to just go home until I either felt worse or actually was dying or perhaps even needed an emergency surgery.

Until then, none of the hospital staff at countless hospitals in the twin cities metro had any interest in helping me. I was young, and I had a couple health 'professionals' accuse me of just wanting to get pain killers. Being told that you need to stop being a junkie when you're actually really sick is one of the most infuriating things that can happen. "I am not going to give you more of these" some would say as handing me a prescription for narcotics. Finally I started firing back with, 'yeah well if your peers could actually help me find out what the problem is I wouldn't need these." As they sent me out the door with a bullshit diagnosis and a handful of narcotics. Follow up with your GI. It was mostly infuriating because half the time I didn't take any of these medications after I filled them. I hoarded them because I knew it was only a matter of time before this shit was going to get worse and I'd save it for when the time came.

As I so accurately had predicted, my illness had amplified and I was now in pain 100% of the time. I stopped eating much because every time I did, It resulted in an entire situation where I would be writhing on the floor in pain staring up at the ceiling asking 'why me' as tears streamed out of my eyes for hours afterwards. These times would typically be spent cursing all the doctors comments that had been seared into my brain such as, 'it's just heartburn', or 'you just have gas' or 'looks like you were here recently and we gave you some pain killers, is that what you're here looking for?' Seriously, and I mean this in the most bitchy way possible, Fuck you.

All these bills started going to collections and what was a single mom to do? I worked a retail job, had a two year old, and was helping to support a whole ass man. There was no choice to be made. I had to just stop going to the doctor. At this time It was crystal clear to me that no one was going to help me unless I was actually teeter tottering with the grim reaper. What makes it even worse is that I let it get to that point before anyone actually helped me.

One night I was standing in the kitchen doing dishes after dinner, hoping to finish washing before the pain made its way home in my belly for the night. Spoiler alert: I did not finish washing the dishes in time.

At this time I lived 1200 miles away from my family - in Baltimore, Maryland. A place void of all my family and lifelong friends. I settled my son into bed with my boyfriend's mom and googled the closest hospital in the area. Franklin Square Hospital was only 4 miles from our house, and for those whole four miles I thought for sure I was going to pass out driving from such agonizing pain. I arrived at the emergency room around 7:00 that night. After checking in and being triaged I made my home in the waiting room for hours. I had next to no energy and knew I had to save what little I could for when they called my name to go back to the room. I couldn't get comfortable and was on the verge of tears the whole time. I didn't get called into a room until 11:00 that night.

For three hours I watched kids play on their tablets as their moms lay lethargic next to them in the waiting room chairs. I felt their pain. I watched the homeless be wheeled by me in wheelchairs. I saw concerned mothers of infants and I heard the rustle of ambulances and squeaks of sneakers when patients with gunshot wounds came in.

I saw people there laughing with the people who brought them in. I judged them hard for it. Not for any good reason, aside from the fact that I was miserable and thought everyone else around me should also partake. Laughing in an ER waiting room? Hello some of us would like to be miserable in peace? The waiting room to death should not be this happy, ma'am. Seriously shut up. I wanted to punch each and every one of them in the face.

Fast forward to when I finally did see a doctor around 1:00 that morning. I was desperate. When the doctor entered the room I could immediately tell she was new, likely a resident. I could still see the empathy in her face. I was a case fresh out of a scene from Grey's Anatomy. Like any good drama, I cried while talking to her about my life. I think that's what got to her. I told her my six year previous history of being in and out of doctors and all my symptoms. She put her sterile, freezing cold hospital hand on mine and said, 'don't worry, I won't let you leave here until we figure out what's going on, okay?' It was at that very moment she changed my life forever. I hate that I don't remember her name, but without her I don't know how much longer it would have taken me to get a diagnosis. Six years alone was long enough. If I ever figure out how to get my hands on my giant medical record, her name will be the first I look for.

They took 8 tubes of blood and wheeled me down to a holding space until they could perform a CT. By this time it was after 2:00 in the morning and I was doing the most to stay conscious. My eyes grew heavier with each passing second. At this point I started panicking because I needed to get home before everyone had to go to work in the morning. I needed to be there when my son woke up. It was such a vulnerable feeling, laying in a hospital gurney burrowed along the perimeter of an overcrowded space filled with the sick and dying. Just as I was on the verge of sleep, I was transported away for my CT. There was more waiting. Finally around 5:00 that morning I got my results. The doctor gently patted me on the back, trying not to startle me because I was waltzing in and out of sleep at this point. She looked at me for a second and with kind eyes said, "Well I have some good news and bad news."

Immediately I started spinning the wheel of misfortune in my head to see what terrible thing we could land on. But I paused just long enough to tell her to give me the good news first.

I have since switched up this method and now always take the bad first. I don't know why on mother earth's green planet I would have ever wanted to take the good news first. Always end on the positive note.

She told me that they are quite certain they have found the cause of my pain. Okay yes, this was GREAT news! Now what was it? She said, 'Have you ever heard of Crohn's Disease?'

I had heard of it. In fact, a lady I worked with at the time had it but I didn't really even know what this diagnosis all entailed. I told her exactly that. She told me that it would require further testing to confirm the diagnosis, since there's just not one single test they can do to prove or disprove you have Crohn's.

Cool.
Sounds expensive.

However, with the amount of inflammation in my intestines on the CT I would need to go to a specialist to confirm. She handed me a packet of papers and I thanked her, with tears in my eyes, for helping me.

I grabbed my packet of medical literature and dropped into the light grey interior of my car. And I sobbed. We're talking giant crocodile tears. I rested my head on my steering wheel and watched the tears drip from my eyes, down the steering wheel into my lap, making tiny little wet spots on my sweatpants. It was now about 7:00 in the morning on the east coast, so even earlier at home. I called my mom anyway.

I woke my mom up via phone call to tell her that I have just been diagnosed with a lifelong, potentially debilitating disease. Over the phone.

All I wanted to do at that moment was hug her and hear her tell me that everything was going to be okay. But I was 1200 miles away. Alone. Crying and watching the sun begin it's shift that day as I sat in the parking lot until my eyes were clear enough and my breathing steady enough to put the car into gear and drive away. It was one of the hardest days I've ever had. I did it all alone.

After arriving back home, I took the day off work. There was a new found burst of energy that had come over me. I had to do research to figure out how I would start living this new life. That day I reached the end of the internet looking for information about Crohn's disease. Every webpage said essentially the same thing. Crohn's is an autoimmune disorder that can affect the digestive tract anywhere from mouth to anus, and let me tell you, in severe cases such as mine it does exactly that. It affects my skin, eyes, and my joints. What I didn't realize at the time is that when a webpage says, 'Symptoms, severity and treatment, work to different degrees for everyone.' It's actually code for, they don't know shit about what is going on or why this is the way it is for some people.

There's no cure, no one diet works for everyone, some diets that do work will stop working, there are limited treatments, might be hereditary, might not be, they don't really know. So, essentially they tell you all the terribleness about it, how it can be treated, and basically they don't really know much more about it and that's all the information there is. Also, this lasts forever so buckle up and enjoy the ride.

When I got diagnosed with a lifelong chronic illness at the ripe old age of 24, life looked a lot different the next day. Your whole world gets rocked and you start looking at things from a different perspective. At least I did. I still do to this day. Then the 'what if's' start rolling in. What if I don't get to see my son get married? What if I don't get to meet my grandchildren (should my children choose to have them?), what if I am unable to get this disease under control? What if I poop my pants on a date? What if I have to have a colostomy bag? I could probably write a whole book on the 'what if's' alone… but that seems like a terrible use of time. Plus I wrote it in my head and it's not even that good.

It took me six weeks to get into a specialist. After those six weeks I had to wait another six weeks to have a colonoscopy. My first colonoscopy was a whole experience in itself. The prep is the absolute worst, and it's almost terrifying to go to bed the night before your procedure. I was so scared I was going to wake up swimming in a pile of my own shit. I also shared a bed so that was extra intimidating. However, I am happy to report that was not the case and I felt like it had to be only by some sort of miracle. The second most intimidating part is driving to the procedure. Unless you have a vehicle with a bathroom in it, this is high cause for anxiety. Especially when your anxiety has anxiety. I took the liberty of mapping out how many gas stations were in between home and the clinic because if we had to stop we would only have mere seconds before my brain got the signal and we would have a literal mess on our hands, and probably other places too.

The procedure itself isn't terrible. I have earned the right to say that now because I have had so many. Most of the time you are knocked out when it happens. I have only had two times where I was still conscious, but it wasn't a normal conscious. I have been awake while they pulled growths from inside my body. I watched myself bleed internally momentarily. I watched it all on a video in real time. On more than one occasion. Medical science is wild.

Since that first colonoscopy I have had at least 8 more. I can handle the prep like it's my job now and here's a pro tip: schedule your procedure earlier in the morning because as part of the prep you're not allowed to eat the day before and the hangries can set in rather quickly if you have to be awake. The only thing that sucks is that if you are lucky enough to get a morning appointment, you have to usually wake yourself up early the morning of the procedure just to finish drinking the other half of your prep... and waking up early just to give yourself violent diarrhea is not the most fun reason to get up early ever.

At the time of this writing I am 33 years old. I have been dealing with Crohn's symptoms for more of my life than I haven't now. 17 years of pain and disease management (which are terms I use very loosely, because a lot of the time I can't afford to manage any of it.) The fact that I can say I have done anything for 17 years makes me feel old, but here I am. That's just the stage of life I am in now. It took me 12 years to find a doctor I trusted. All my progress went out the door with the announcement of his retirement this last year.

My version of this disease is still not under control. Some days staring at my pill box and giving myself injections is hard, when I can actually afford my prescriptions. It's also hard not being able to stare your pill box because you can't afford your medications, despite paying over $500 a month for medical insurance.

Dealing with the fatigue and medication side effects is hard, I'm tired a lot, and overall I just feel crummy a lot of the time. The pain affects my mood and that makes me feel guilty on top of the mom guilt I typically feel anyway. It makes me anxious, tired, and takes a toll on my mental health. There are days I don't want to get out of bed or even have the energy to shower. There are times I make plans but have to flake because of my illness - which I believe has caused the downfall of some of my friendships. But even so, everyday I get up and do the best I can and that's something to be proud of. Even if my best falls below my incredibly high Virgo expectations. I lived to see another day. I was able to kiss my babies goodnight again, laugh, breathe in fresh air, fall in love a little more, and do things that make me forget about how much I hurt sometimes.

That, my friends, is the real gift.

Jess Is Sus...

I suffer from what I can only imagine is one of the worst cases of imposter syndrome. I find that I have a desire to learn and do all these things, which I do, but then feel as though I don't *actually* earn the privilege of being able to bestow such a title.

For example, I paint watercolor pieces. People order them from me, purchase them from me, and display my artwork in their homes. I've known people to give my pieces as gifts even. I have my own website and I designed the cover of this book. But yet when I want to call myself an artist I feel like I haven't quite earned it.

This thought brings me back to being a kid. Do you remember just playing outside with your peers and during pretend play you declare your title? "I am the mom but I am also an artist." We declared who and what we were before we'd even begun to go through the motions of being such a thing. We made an unfaltering decision as who we are before we had even begun. We rarely consulted with anyone, because we already knew who we wanted to be.

When and why does that stop? When does our confidence in our abilities and ourselves as a whole just disappear? How do we fix it?

I want to fix it for everyone.

One of my favorite running jokes I have is between my sister and our husbands. The gist of it is, my sister and I are essentially identical in the way we think and the way we act. Our husbands love that they can bond over a potential scenario and predict exactly to a T how both my sister and I will behave.

They're right 100% of the time. Then, my sister and I explode into big belly laughs, and explain our way as to why we react the way we do and our answer and logic is always the exact same. It's the nurture in us, it's how we grew up. I find this so fascinating and I love that sisterly bond about us.

Love you, Beck.

One night my sister and I had the following conversation regarding our small businesses and feeling like imposters.

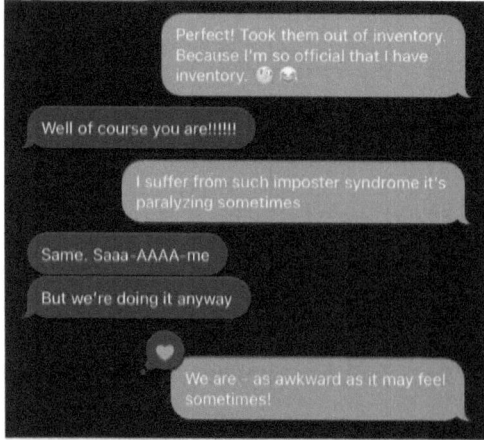

This conversation has stuck with me since it happened. Anytime I start talking down to myself about how I'm 'not technically' an artist or a writer, I go back to this conversation.

If my sister were to come to me doing all the incredible things that she does and tell me she doesn't feel like she's able to label herself as such, what would I say to her? After all, if I truly believe we are the same person then that is how I should be talking to myself, ya feel me? If we have ourselves convinced and our husbands can predict how we'll react to a T, there has to be some truth to it, right?

If negative self-talk is something you participate in, when I tell you that talking nicely or even neutral to yourself will change your life I am not kidding you. If I hadn't started talking neutral to myself and about myself, you wouldn't have this book in your beautiful hands. I would not be an artist, a writer, nor would I have personal goals. I would have been too scared to start something.

For years I was.

The process of analyzing thoughts and using your mind to your advantage, especially with mental illness does incredible things for your outlook on life. It shapes how you feel about yourself, and finding purposeful activities. It is the baby seed from which you will flourish. But you have to nurture yourself in order for that to happen. Are we sensing a recurring theme here yet?

In my experience, at first most things are uncomfortable. You don't know how to be, how to act, or how to do a thing. It's weird! It's even more awkward if someone is watching you.

This includes retitling yourself as something you've never been before. Of course there are going to be bumps and bruises along the way. You may take a digger and skin your knee even. But if you constantly think you need to accomplish more, or do more, or you haven't done enough to call yourself an artist or a writer or whatever it is that you want to be - I invite you to question yourself. What would you say to a friend who was saying the same thing to you, despite all their accomplishments? We tend to be our own worst critics and a lot harder on ourselves than we are to our loved ones. This happens for no actual good reason.

I hope you all have that friend or that sibling or that someone you feel you have connected with on a deeper level. The ones who you go to when you need advice or when you need a night to vent or someone to eat snacks and smoke joints with. I hope there is someone in your life that makes you laugh so hard your belly hurts and your cheeks ache from smiling so much. Think of how you would talk to them, and then start talking to yourself that way.

See you Later

In the year that shall not be named (aka 2020) I don't need to tell you that shit was wild. Rumor has it if you say that number three times fast in a mirror the world will implode on itself, but I have yet to try that out. We took blow after blow collectively as humans, as a nation then on painful, individual levels where we shared in our misery with each other via social media.

One of the personal attacks of the year that shall not be named on my family was the passing of my grandfather. I was incredibly fortunate to make it to the age of 32 before I had to attend the celebration of life for one of my own grandparents. My experience I am sure is skewed to a degree because of COVID so there were more policy restrictions in place than would be in a standard nursing home, hospital or funeral in regards to visiting. My grandpa's death hit different. Like many, I suffered through thoughts of my loved one spending much of his last days being alone. No one was able to hold his hand or rub his forehead while he slept like I had done with family members who have passed before him. As a granddaughter I was robbed of being able to hug my grandfather. I was isolated from my grandmother in what were sure to be some of her worst days. Where instead of being surrounded by family in our time of loss, she was also alone. We couldn't have that last conversation with my grandfather. What if he was having a 'good day' and he thinks no one cares to come see him? We love you Grandpa, they just can't let us in.

The last time I saw my grandfather was the year prior. We went to visit him at the nursing home. He was in an out of any understanding of what was going on. He would make jokes one minute about how terrible his memory was and then in the next sentence talk about something completely different. He told me that he wanted me to come around more. His last memory of me was when I was six years old. He told me that so much had changed since he saw me last and that I grew into a beautiful young woman. He thought he hadn't seen me since I was six. That was the first heart shatter of the visit.

When it was time to go, my grandpa went to his room and put his jacket on. He thought he was coming home with us. I nervously looked around at the staff, to make sure they knew we were going to need some assistance in getting him to not actually leave the building with us. My anxiety skyrocketed. We got to the doors and the nurse came over. She grabbed my grandfather by the hand and said, "Hey Clarence! How about we let the women and children out first?" My grandfather of course agreed, and my grandma reached up and kissed him goodbye with tears in her eyes. I died inside. We walked out the door and the nurse shut the heavy door behind us before my grandpa could get out the door.

We all stood in the lobby and sobbed. I held my grandmother as she cried. My kids' faces indicated a sadness and heartbreak that I have never seen. Seeing that look in all three of them at the same time was psychological torture.

It was winter, the sidewalks were icy and blanketed with a layer of snow. Once I loaded all the kids and helped my weeping grandmother into the car. I got in and as I looked up out of my windshield. I saw my grandpa standing there in the window. Still with his coat and gloves on. He waved at us. My heart was absolutely wrecked. We all sat in the car and cried together. Driving away from that nursing home was one of the most heartbreaking things I've ever done.

My grandma and grandpa got married when they were 17 and 18 respectively. From what I gather, my grandmother and her mother didn't get along. When I called my grandma out of a fit of surprise to confirm that she did get married at such a young age, (which I only found out about because I found her marriage certificate online while doing some genealogy research) she told me, "Oh yes, my mother and I didn't get along, so grandpa came along and he saved me from all of that."

I never really clarified what 'all of that' meant. If she was willing to talk about it, she would have. I did, however, catch a glimpse of sourness in her tone. Bonnie is too much of an angel to ever speak ill of anyone, no matter how they wronged her. She'd never articulate those feelings through her words into the atmosphere, but her tone will tell you everything you need to know about how she really feels. I have always loved that about her. As much as her tone and facial expressions tell you when she detests something, when she speaks of love and joy, you get to feel that from her too. She's the perfect yin and yang.

My grandmother spent every waking minute of her life with my grandfather since she was essentially a child. From going to school, to raising a family, to traveling, being involved in the community, and just overall being good people, retiring to a home overlooking a lake... they did it all together. They lived a whole life, they grew old together and never gave up on each other. I cannot tell you how much it broke me inside to know their love story earthside was going to end this way. They lived to love and take care of each other, and at the end they had to love each other from the most distance they've ever had to experience with one another. Excuse me while I sweep up the pieces of my heart off the dirty floor.

The day my grandfather passed away will forever be ingrained into my brain. Not because I was there, or got to say my final 'see you laters', or hold his hand one more time - but because we all couldn't. Much like his last days, we all had to face this giant without the direct support of the family that connected us, and that was a tough experience for me. Not being able to run to each other made the hurt sting that much more.

The next few days run together because of the lack of sleep, amount of ativan, and quantity of weed smoked were way out of proportion in comparison with my standard days. I must've sensed this was coming because the night before his passing I ended up in the back of an ambulance having a panic attack that left me unable to control my bowels, feel my limbs or control my breathing. I was in the ER for several hours, prescribed some ativan, and was sent on my merry way (because again, not dying). Little did I know, we were just getting started. I have always been able to sense things before or shortly after they happen. This time was no different.

As the dust was settling, my phone rang. My dad had called me a day later and said, 'grandma was wondering if you'd want to write a little something and read it at the funeral.' I didn't even give myself time to think because if I would had I knew I would have backed out. I couldn't let her down like that. "Yeah... I can do that. I'll write something up and have it ready."

I hung up the phone and opened my notes app. I reached back into the memory bank and started writing down some of the recollections I wanted to include in my portion of the ceremony. It was only mere moments before one of my children saw me comfortable and needed something. So as the day went on I jotted down different phrases or memories I wanted to relay as they popped up. I wrote them all down as the day went on between my run of the mill tasks. My husband was kind enough to take care of the big things like, making sure the kids were fed, and booking a hotel for when we had to travel to the funeral in the coming days. While he was being productive, I was busy lashing out at people at Barnes and Noble (grief is weird, but also - she approached me first) and doing non-essential tasks like, organizing the cleaners under the kitchen sink and washing the walls.

I absolutely did not believe that I was going to be able to get up in front of people and read emotional things in front of emotional people with my grandfather in the room in a casket next to me. I have been to a number of funerals and I always sob. Like an infant. I can't even watch dog videos in my social media feeds without tearing up and don't even get me started on the military service members surprising their kids or moms or families by showing up at their loved ones school or work. Listen, what I'm trying to convey is that I'm not good at *not* crying. This was going to be a bitch of a task and I didn't know how I was going to do this, but I had to figure it out for Grandma.

Like most depressed creatives, I put off writing probably the most important speech of my life until about 12 hours before the actual event. Which also coincidentally coincided with the time I should be getting some restful sleep to promote clear thinking and attentive sharpness for the day ahead. But alas, a bonfire, some hard apple cider, and anxiety medication sounded like a better idea to me. "Did you start writing your speech yet?" Nick asked me, over the glow of the little fire pit our hotel had out front. "No," I responded. "I have to do that tonight before I go to bed." I knew he already knew the answer before he asked the question. He was more or less nudging me in the way of, Jess... it's time to write so that you can get some sleep so we can face tomorrow. I knew what he was doing. I was being stubborn. Writing meant I had to write about my grandfather in the past tense for the first time. It felt so final. There is no more 'my grandpa is' it was now, 'my grandpa was' and that was a reference I had never used before. It was never one I had to verbalize in a room full of people who would be staring at me with pain in their hearts and tears in their eyes. People who carried love in their heart for a man who meant so much to so many people. No pressure, though.

We got the kids settled into the hotel room. Five of us sleeping in one room is about as nightmarish as I manifested it would be. I never feel good about the sleeping situation when someone is on a cot and people who are not used to sharing beds are sharing beds. But, if that's the worst thing that happens to my kids, let it be a lesson in being resilient.

Once everyone was snoring, I went and grabbed my laptop from the other side of the room. Also, I highly do not recommend obstacle course-ing over your children in a room in the dark that you're not already familiar while simultaneously trying to not wake them up. It was 11:14 PM before I got any words down on that paper. By 2:00 I had finished editing and felt good about what I had written. I still had no idea how I was going to be able to verbalize these deeply personal words and memories (which are usually kept private in notebooks scattered throughout my home) in front of a room of people at one of my most vulnerable moments. But, that was a task I would figure out later. I took an Ativan and I went to bed.

Cut to a few hours later and we were at the funeral home. Feeling a whole lot of feelings, I sat in the front pew and was reading over my speech as people filed through the line to say a final goodbye to my grandfather. I purposefully positioned myself in front of the picture boards because I wanted to hear what memories got triggered by the displays. "He was such a good man," "He loved (fill in the blank)" "This picture is from when we ___". I needed these things. I put the final edits on my writing and saved it in my email. The next time I opened that email would be the time I was reading it in front of a crowd.

I had reached into my purse to grab yet another tissue and something to help my anxiety. The folded funeral program had fallen out of my bag when I pulled out the other things. I opened it and read it for the first time. I looked at the nature photo on the front of the program for longer than I would have if I had seen the artwork anywhere else out in the world. I opened the pamphlet and in big bold letters was my grandpa's name, birth and death date, followed by a poem. Anyone who has been to a funeral is probably quite familiar with the layout. Also made a small note to self to create my own funeral pamphlet and put it in my death request stuff - because I want my life to be personalized by me down to the very last drop. I do weird things like that.

The funeral was a blur, partly because I was trying to quiet cry and there were so many tears in my eyes I couldn't see - but also because the feeling of heartbreak surrounded me as I listened to my grandparents wedding song and watched my grandmother fall apart as it played. When my time to speak approached, I opened the email and made my way up to the podium. I didn't wear my glasses because 1. I was crying as though my face had turned into a natural spring and 2. Because if people were blurry it'd be easier for me to read my speech if I couldn't see the eyes staring back at me. Sometimes having not the best vision is helpful.

I put a disclaimer on my speech before I started. Not that I had to explain my emotion at a funeral, but for some reason it always makes me feel more comfortable to tell people I am going to be a wreck before I actually become it. Kind of a warning, if you will. Before I made it through the first paragraph I had to stop and catch my breath. My dad offered some words of encouragement over the silence that had fallen over the room as I fell apart. Overwhelmed with emotion, I finally made it through. I could add ``Deliver a Eulogy" to my resume of really hard things I've done that I never thought I'd have to do. If you don't have a list like this, it can be very inspiring if you ever need a reminder of all the hard things you've endured. However, if you're negative minded this can be more hurtful than helpful so just make sure you're in the right headspace for that list should you choose to create it.

We traveled an extra hour and a half to the burial, and after the casket was lowered into the ground I sat there for a little longer. I didn't know how to feel or what to really do after that. It feels so strange that you just... put your loved one in the ground and then go about your life. It still seems so strange to me. I left a piece of my heart in that cemetery that day. What I do know is that I'll likely only ever visit that cemetary once more in my life, and that day will be equally as terrible if not more so than the day I just had.

The Actual Most Important Never Ending Chapter

Jackson Lyle, Jaida Lynn, and Elizabeth Kay - the absolute loves, purpose, and my entire souls being in this life:

As I sit here and write this chapter, tears stream down my face. Sure, I am only 33 years old and potentially I have a lot of life left to live. But god dammit do I know deep down in my soul that the three of you are absolutely my purpose for being here. I never understood love without conditions until you. I never had a purpose, a reason to be better until you. With each of you came more and more power. More drive to do better, and to be better… to understand and to care more and to show you that this world can really be as terrible or as wonderful as you want it to be. Both options are out there and both are available to you. It's up to you to decide what you want.

I hope if I leave you with anything in this lifetime, it's that you know what it is to love something fiercely and to follow your dreams. I hope that you know it is to never stop learning and never stop growing. Don't get comfortable. Learn and expand as much as you can. Interact and know many types of people, but also stay rooted in yourself. Set boundaries and don't betray you. Your most important relationship is the one you have with yourself. Make you happy first. Follow your instincts. Don't be afraid to come off rude if you're uncomfortable. Stop means stop the first time.

Jackson - The one who made me a mom. What a ride it's been, buddy. I made a promise to you the night you were born as I was counting your perfect little fingers, and your chubby little toes, that no matter what situation we would find ourselves in, I was going to make sure we were going to make it. It was going to be me and you little dude, and I was going to figure it out and I wasn't going to let you down. It was the scariest promise I had ever made because I didn't have a plan, and I didn't know that I could actually keep it. But I was going to make damn sure I figured out a way. You've been there through my every stumble and every faceplant I've taken in this life. We've been in the trenches together and yet here we are. You're my rock. I hope you never stop giving me hugs every time you walk in the room and I hope you never let this world harden your heart. You're incredible, you're a helper and you always want to do the right thing. You're the protector of your sisters. You've always fought for the underdog and as a mother, I hope you know how proud that makes me.

Jaida - My little carbon copy. The one who has marched to the beat of her own drum since the day she decided she wanted to be born, three weeks early. You, my darling, have taught me so much about myself, but about life in general. You have taught me love, patience, and what it's like to raise a copy of myself. You challenge me and sometimes we butt heads. On the flip side, we also laugh until we can't breathe and we have deep, soul soothing conversations. Our sense of humor is the same, and you can tell a 'that's what she said' joke better than anyone I know. You're fun, you're kind, you're so smart, and girl you are going to achieve whatever you put your mind to. You are committed to fairness and justice for all. I can't wait to see what you do in this world, babe. I know it's going to be incredible.

Ellie - My sweet, sweet girl. You are the little candy cherry on top to our family. You care so deeply about others and are my nature companion. I love spending time with you and our conversations when we're walking through the magical woods. Your mind is creative, beautiful, and generous. You love your family with every ounce of your being and your curiousness about life and whimsical outlook makes life look so magical. You make us laugh, and your snuggles warm my soul. You're thoughtful, always taking others feelings into account, and your imagination is unmatched. We are so lucky to have you.

You all have smiles that light up a room, laughs that make my heart dance, and have shown me what love is. No matter what this life may bring to me - the greatest honor of my entire life has been to be your mother. No matter how 'successful' the world sees me or how much money I make. I would give it all up in a heartbeat, without hesitation, for you. You've been my greatest teachers, and you've shown me who I am and who I want to be. You've taught me how to love deeply and unconditionally. You've taught me how to stare fear in the eye and do shit anyway. You are my fire, my light, my whole reason for everything I do. I was put on this earth to be your mother - to teach you fairness, justice, and love despite the circumstances. I hope you always scoff at societal standards and do what's right in your heart to do. Trust yourself. You were born perfect, my loves. I owe my life to my babies and I hope you know that every choice I made was made with your best interest at my soul's core.

It truly has been my highest honor to be able to be your mom. Even your mother, the Virgo, wasn't perfect. (but I mean, probably pretty close)

You've added a level of richness and beauty to this life that I've never experienced before you arrived. Find the little things everyday that make you happy and write them down. Disconnect - find hobbies that don't include electronics. Don't stop reading books. Tell people how you feel. Never stop fighting for what is right.

But most importantly:

You are your biggest asset. I hope you love yourself though the good and the bad. And if by chance you lose your way - I will be here to remind you. Always remember, ain't nobody ever gonna love you like your momma.

Truth or Likes?

There's this funny thing that starts happening when you begin the healing process. You'll come across toxic behavior that you, yourself used to participate in. You'll do the work to heal that inner trauma, but then you'll see it in your friends and family. When this happens, it's so readily obvious and you're able to pick up on these toxic traits the second they happen. While sometimes this can look amusing, it also can be very difficult to watch people perform the way they do. As an elder millennial, you see this far too much in the age of social media. Sometimes even in your Facebook memories which most of the time leaves me cringing.

How many times have you been that person who perfectly poses their kids or bribes them with a toy or a snack if they just pretend to like each other for just one more photo? How many filters have we added to photos in our social media lifespan? We delete photos of ourselves with our friends and family because of our chin. How many times have we fallen victim to posting our highlight reels on social media when it feels like our life is falling apart in real time?

I had a conversation with my therapist about social media and the impact it has to the downfall of my mental health. On weeks where I feel most anxious or weeks where I throw the most lavish of pity parties for myself, it's no coincidence that those are the days I spend more time on social media. It's hard though, right? To not check in on what the people from high school or your friends are doing? What the latest celebs are promoting? I was more concerned about putting myself down. I thought about how 'less of' a fun mom, good wife, artist, writer, or whatever else I was considering being at the time. When it comes down to it, I was doing these things for no good reason. Just because it was available and something for me to do. Talk about a detrimental waste of my own time and potential.

To be quite honest I was nervous to post on social media - being a recovering people pleaser and taking a firm stand on something to my whole audience of 350 people felt scary. What if someone has something negative to say? What if people don't agree with me? What if someone says something and hurts my feelings?

My past has contorted me into forms I didn't know I could get into. I have healed in places I didn't know there were gaping wounds, and I participated in more therapy sessions then I have cumulatively up until this point in my life. I started sharing more and more about myself, and guess what happened? NOTHING. Sure, my number of likes went down, and maybe my number of friends or followers decreased, but I couldn't tell you who those people were that no longer found me worthy of following. Do you know what posting more of my truth did? It opened the door for real conversations with people going through the same thing. It started a dialogue with people that I hadn't talked to for years, experiencing the same things that I had and we bonded over these scenarios together. It brought me closer to *my* people. People I didn't even know were struggling or hurting, and I got to be there for them and it felt unifying in a way that was unfamiliar, maybe a little awkward, but it also felt nice to not be completely and utterly alone.

If you're following someone and their posts make you feel like shit, do yourself a favor and unfollow that person. If you're questioning your worth after seeing how other people parent, it's time to disconnect. If your feed isn't inspiring you to put your phone down and learn or do something new or make you feel good about the words and images you're ingesting it's time to make some radical changes to your timeline. Curate your timeline so that it serves you. Your timelines should fill you with love, and inspire you to get off your phone and get out there and change the world. Maybe add some content that makes you laugh. Exchange your neutrality for truth, and you'll find the people that are meant for you. Not only will it do wonders for your mental health, but it'll also catapult you into a world of self care and excitement about your own goals that you can use to share and inspire others and receive genuine support.

At the end of the day I find complacency incredibly boring. You are the author of your story - I hope what you're digitally publishing for the world to see aren't face tuned and filtered into oblivion photos, trading your truth for neutrality likes. Find your voice and be loud with it. Find what you love and run towards it with a vehement passion. Do what makes you happy, do what's easiest for you. After all, this is your crazy, beautiful life and from what I hear - it's short. Find your passions before you get arthritis in your hands or need surgery on your back that prevents you from doing the things you love. When you find yourself scrolling on your phone mindlessly you can yell, "THIS ISN'T GETTING ME TO MY GOALS" and put your phone to bed and do something productive. This is my favorite method, because I announce it to my household. They then find it fun to keep me accountable if they find me scrolling again on my phone in the short moments after my declaration of annoyance with myself. It's a fun game for all of us, and by all of us I mean everyone else who gets to call me out for sleeping on my goals.

If I can offer you any advice, it's to decrease the amount of time you spend on social media. Don't compare yourself to literally anyone, because no two people are the same, and thank goodness they aren't. Spend your time doing things you like, instead of looking for clout on the internet. The only validation you need is from yourself.

Your most important likes are from yourself, darling.

Intuition

Before we get into this chapter, I want to be fully transparent that this chapter talks about sexual assault. If this is something that's difficult for you - please skip this section. It's not imperative that you read it to understand the rest of the book.

Sometimes I like to joke around and say I manifested my own Crohn's Disease because I ignored all my gut feelings my whole life. Which, to be honest I am still really open to this being the root cause considering Crohn's supposed to be hereditary and there's no one else in my family that has Crohn's Disease. I mean, all I'm saying is that it's not out of the realm of possibility in my world.

During this disheveled stroll through our cosmic journey as humans there are times we experience situations where our body is communicating something before our mind is. There is a force strong enough to try and physically steer you away from a situation before your mind can really catch up. Or, you'll have a feeling so strong after a thought that pushes you to investigate something further. This can only happen though if you slow down enough to be in tune with what your being is trying to communicate to you.

If I could take all the red flags I've experienced in my life, I would be able to make several parachutes as large as the ones we used to play with in gym class in elementary school. Remember how huge those things felt as a kindergartener? We could fit 25 snot nosed kids under that thing and still have room for more. That's how big my red flag parachutes would be.

It was the tail end of my high school year. I was gearing up to work full time and get ready for the real world. I worked at a store in the mall near my house. I had only been working there for a couple of weeks when I was asked to help set up and open a store at the Mall of America. Several of us filled in until they were able to get their own staff trained and ready to go. I really don't know why I agreed, probably because I wanted the money. Literally everything else about that situation I really didn't want to do. The commute was going to be horrendous. With traffic it took me almost an hour to get to where I needed to be - which was a vast contrast from the ten minute commute I was used to. I would be working doubles on the weekends and leaving school early to go to work as part of a program our school offered during the week. I would be up with the sunrise and crawling into bed hours after the sun had set.

There was a man who worked there that all the older ladies seemed to enjoy. They would laugh and flirt and overall just have a grand old time getting things set up, bonding over gemstones that cost more than anything else I had ever held in my hands. He gave me the creeps. I only spoke to him if I absolutely needed to. He would smile at me from across the store and I would smile back in an effort to be polite, but then look away and try to direct my attention to tasks or cleaning or talking to some of the people closer to my age just to avoid him.

One night, I was working a closing shift with this guy. The night couldn't have gone by any slower than it already was. We started closing up the store, putting jewelry back in the safe, taking inventory and double checking that every safe and glass case was locked. He closed the front gate to the store and I said, 'Have a good night!" and started walking towards the side of the mall where my car was parked. If you've never been to the Mall of America, they have two large parking structures, one on the east side and one on the west side. Each level of the parking ramp is blazened with a bold color, and named after a state. There wasn't a designated area for staff parking at the time, or if there was I wasn't aware of it.

"Where are you going?" this question caught me off guard. "I am going home, I have school in the morning." He smiled and said, "You can't get to your car from that way anymore once the mall is closed." I was naive, and I believed him. "What? really?" I stammered, now trying to figure out how I was going to get back to my car without having to walk a thousand miles around the mall. "Come with me, I will bring you to your car." I agreed on the outside, but on the inside there were alarm bells going off. I attributed their presence to just being nervous from being around new people a lot. We started walking towards the parking ramp that his car was in. He was making small talk and I was just responding with short answers, focusing on just getting to my car. I was tired. I wanted to go home.

We made it out to the parking lot, his car chirping as he pushed the unlock button. I fell into the passenger seat and immediately put my seat belt on. "I am parked on Nevada", I said. In my head it sounded a lot more like, 'get me the fuck out of here'. "Okay" he paused for what felt like an eternity. "Hey...Do you want to go get a drink?"

I scoffed at him, "No, I am not old enough so I can't go to a bar anyway."

He offered to buy me a drink and I told him no, that I wasn't comfortable drinking under age and driving home. He then said, 'Well, you can come with me then." I didn't want to. I should have gotten out of the car at that very moment. He pulled out of the parking spot and drove to a bar across the street from the mall. He asked if I wanted to sit outside and I told him, only for a minute, because I really need to get home. He ordered two drinks, pushing one in front of me once the wait staff was out of view. I pushed it back towards him and told him no. I sat there while he finished one of the beers in front of him. I asked him if he would please bring me to my car. He chugged half of the second beer, and stood up and said, 'lets go.' A wave of relief washed over me. I was finally going to get to go home and far away from this guy..

We got into the car and I buckled my seat belt for the short drive across the street. We entered the parking ramp and he passed the level I was parked on. "Oh, this is the level right here". A sinister smile appeared on his face. "Lets go to the top". My heart sank. Why was this fool not listening to me? I had homework to do and it was already late. My mom would be calling soon to find out where I was.

He drove to the top of the parking ramp and shut the car off. I sat in the passenger seat, still with my seat belt on - in an effort to make it clear I was not getting out of the car. I was nervous, this wasn't right. I could feel every muscle and organ of my body shaking in fear. He removed his seat belt and leaned over toward me. He put his hands on me. I clenched every muscle in my body. "What are you doing? No... stop" I started crying. "Stop... Stop... Stop" was all I could scream. No one was around. No one could hear me.

I don't remember much of the rest of the details, and even if I did I wouldn't write them here. All you need to know is that I was sexually assaulted in that parking structure.

Before finally being brought back to my car. I texted my mom letting her know I was on my way home. I knew that if she heard my voice she'd know something happened, and I couldn't deal with that on my drive home. I sat in my car and cried like I had never cried before. I gathered my bearings, and called my best friend. I never told her what had happened that night (until just this year, actually) but I just couldn't be alone on that car ride home. I needed someone to talk to about normal teenage things, and -like she always does- she delivered. Not knowing the absolute hero she was to me at that point in time.

It took me 15 years to be able to talk about this assault out loud. I don't remember his name, what car he was driving, what day it was, or any of those details. I don't know where he was from originally, and I don't recall if I ever worked with him again. For a long, long time I felt as though the whole situation was my fault. I didn't do enough, I didn't make enough noise, I wasn't rude enough, I should've called someone. I could 'should' myself to death in this scenario, and at times I have. I know now that it wasn't my fault. It's never the victim's fault and this is a hill I am willing to die on. Not just for my sake, but for the sake of anyone who's ever had to experience something so outrightly heinous. Or anyone who has a daughter.

It didn't matter what I was wearing. I was in 'professional' work attire.

It didn't matter where I was. I was at work.
It didn't matter if I said no, it didn't matter that I asked him to stop. I asked him to bring me to my car.
All I was trying to do was go home.

Was there more I could have done to get out of the situation? Probably. But you can miss me with all those suggestions because until you're (hopefully never) in that situation, you don't know how you're going to react. If at any time someone trusts you enough to talk to you about a situation like this, please don't ask the person why they didn't do something differently. Just listen. Just be there for them.

Moral of the story is, you don't owe anyone 'nice.' Especially if you're feeling anxious or like something isn't vibing. You don't owe an explanation after using the word 'no', and you sure as hell don't need to end your feelings with an 'lol.' Put your feelings and interests first. This world can be so dangerous.
We need to get rid of this notion that the more and more we, as women, sacrifice ourselves or our feelings for others makes us 'better' or perceived as 'nicer'. In this (and many other previous situations) I ignored my own intuitions in the name of being polite; in the name of being perceived as 'nice'. I kept quiet in times where I should have demanded answers & respect. I didn't ask for help when I should have.

What I'm saying is always trust your gut. Your gut knows things that your mind will grasp later.

A Dark Night

This chapter by far is going to be one of the hardest for me to write. Simply because the story is derived from one of the nights that I didn't think I was going to live to see daylight the next morning. If you know of anyone, or if you suspect that anyone you know is in danger, please talk to them. Text their siblings, call their parents, message their cousin on Facebook. Be all in until you know the abused is in a safe space. But most of all, be there for them.

Being a survivor of domestic abuse I can tell you, all it takes is to know there is just ONE rock solid person you can rely on. As the cliche goes, 'it only takes one.' A lot of time these people are mentally beaten down with no self esteem. They have been distanced from those they love and trust in the beginning of the relationship. The abuser makes the victim think no one cares about or wants them. Believe me when I tell you, we believe it.

 The victim needs to know there's one safe place... just one safe person, just one that they can go to and trust. I know what a lot of you are thinking, "Just call the police". While for some people that may be an option, from my experience it usually is the least effective option. The police can't and won't do anything unless they find you beaten and bloody on the floor. They remove one party from the situation, maybe take them to jail for a night or two, and then the abuser is released. Filled with a new type of rage, and a whole lot more to be upset about. The police will tell you to find a safer place to stay, and get a restraining order. That's where their advice and helpfulness ends. Also not actually helpful when you have no money or no other place to go. So you wait. You wait for what's to come. It's never pretty.

If you can't be that person - find someone who can or provide the victim with resources physically away from their homes because trust me when I tell you, they are already in survival mode. Once they step out of the door of danger, they're already thinking about what they're going to say or do when they come back. They expect to come back. Most of the time, we do come back. We do this because their self esteem has been worn down so far that they don't think they deserve better. They're rehearsing their apology in their being, curating the response to their partner when they find out the victim has left. Abused people typically can't look up resources or reach out for help for themselves a lot of the time due to tracking devices or other means of surveillance. Yes this is real, yes this happens.

Here is a trigger warning - this part of the story has to do with assault, and is only a moment in time of what this year long relationship was.

My phone lifted me from the depths of my dream.. "Hello?' I answered. "What... are you sleeping? I need you to come get me." On the other end of the line was my ever so charming boyfriend of three whole months.

"Of course I'm sleeping, it's 2:00 in the morning and I have to work at 8:00."

"Oh shit… come get me. I want to lay next to you and my kid." he slurred. I could basically smell the alcohol on his breath through the phone the way I've smelled it before nearly every night. Something that my new found morning sickness was already awakened by.

"By the time I get there, it's going to be damn near 3:00, it'll take another half hour to get back to your aunt's house, and I'll have to leave by 6 to get back to my house by 7 so I can be ready and to work by 8. I am pregnant and I am exhausted. I'm sure you're with someone who can take you home."

"Are you seriously going to not come and get me?" His question was so accusatory that anything other than an immediate response of 'I'm on my way' I knew wasn't going to fly.

"Ugh… I'll be right there. Where are you?"

He gave me the name of the nightclub. It was Halloween. Since I was only 18, there were certain clubs in the Twin Cities area that were 21+ that I couldn't get into. He had informed me that he was going to a 21+ club that night. I already knew in my gut that he was going to be with someone else that night. I never got concrete proof - but knowing what I know about him now… it definitely wasn't because he loved me that he chose to abandon his newly pregnant girlfriend of three months to hang out at a place I wasn't legally allowed to enter at the time.

My first pregnancy wasn't easy. I was consistently nauseous for the first four months of being pregnant. I threw up like clockwork every 15 minutes for three hours every morning. I could time it perfectly. With that being said, I wasn't particularly interested in going out for halloween that year, however my friend had talked me into it and we went to a party where I knew no one and met some of her friends. I ended up getting really tired and she took me home where I passed out. I had texted my boyfriend telling him I was going to sleep and of course received zero response. So sweet. That is, until that phone call that woke me up a couple hours later.

Like I had predicted, I didn't get to where he was until about 3 in the morning. I could smell the alcohol permeating out of his pores as he drunkenly fell into my car. He sloppily slammed the car door and looked at me, pointed forward and said, 'drive', as if I was some sort of chauffeur. At that point I didn't care. Just get me to a bed so I can go the fuck back to sleep.

I asked him how his night was, and he said, 'Oh my god... it was SO GOOD. There were all these HOT girls there, grinding up all over me."

I felt my face get hot. I have never felt my heart sink down into my gut so fast. What the fuck. By no means have I ever dated literally any winners in my life up to this point, but by far this was the most disrespected I had ever felt. This was a new level of disappointment and heartbreak that I had yet to experience. Yet here it was, in all its glory. A pain that I never even knew existed. He said this to hurt me, like most things he said when he was drinking and angry. This mother fucker just woke me up, made me drive an hour to pick his sorry ass up, and now he's going to speak to me, his pregnant 'girlfriend' this way? Before I could even finish processing the thought, tears projected from my eyes. They left a trail of what I can only assume was salt as the tears evaporated off my flushed cheeks.

He giggled a little bit and through a smile said, "why the fuck are you crying?"

"You're seriously going to ask me that right now?" I responded, through my tears. Never taking the gaze off the road. I could feel his eyes burning into the side of my face.

He laughed some more. "You are such a child. You can just bring me to my aunt's house and go home."

I started slowing the car down and pulling over on the freeway. I had enough. This is not how I ever expected to be treated by my child's "father".

Panicked, he started asking me "What are you doing? What are you doing?" His gaze flickered back to the rear window to see if there was a cop or maybe an ambulance to explain why I was pulling over.

I stopped on the side of the road, next to a concrete median on my left. It was dark, and the streetlights dimly lit the street with an orange hue. When I had stopped, the tears in my eyes were thick & heavy, and my vision was blurry. It was at this moment I was on the verge of having a panic attack, but at the time I didn't know that. I took a deep breath and I put both of my hands on the wheel, pushed my foot into the brake as hard as I could, as if my body was bracing for impact. I looked forward and said as calmly as I could, 'get out... of my car.'

"What are you doing? I am not getting out of this car. You need to drive." He said, almost sober-like.

I closed my eyes and felt the tears slide down my cheeks again. I repeated, 'You need to get the fuck out of my car."

"Look I am sorry okay. Can you just drive? It's 3:00 in the morning and you're not just going to leave me on the side of the road..."

"Why would you say something like that to me?" I interrupted him. I was so confused and heartbroken that I didn't even want to look at him. I didn't want to sit next to him or be near him. I was nauseated. I wanted him out of my car and at this point, I wanted to go home.

"I was just mad, okay? You were all dressed up all cute for Halloween and then you went out with your friends. I was just jealous and that's why I went where I did. I drank too much and I'm sorry."

This was a bullshit apology but I was young and naive at the time. I accepted this cringeworthy performance. I know, I know... gross. Believe me, I learned from this experience.

I turned on my signal, not really sure why as the road was completely empty. I started to merge back on to the highway. We got about a mile down the road and all was quiet. Out of what seemed like nowhere, he slammed his forearm down on my leg. I tried to back off the gas pedal to slow down, but he was of course, much stronger than I was. I started screaming, telling him to stop. The car went faster with the pressure on my leg. He jerked the wheel across several lanes of traffic and yelled into my face, "Don't you ever pull some shit like that with me again. I will kill you, me, and this baby - I don't give a fuck. You really want to be upset? You want something to cry over? Maybe you should smell my fingers…" His face was inches from my own, and it was with that comment I thought for sure I was going to die. He jerked the steering wheel. I braced my whole body in response to what I can assume was either the feeling of my heart breaking to the point of death, of terror, or trauma of what was to come to my body from whatever I was about to crash into.

As my car got closer and closer to the center median I kicked on the emergency brake. Thank god for whatever instinct that was because I don't even know what took over me to know to do that in that very moment. I can't place where my emergency brake even was in that car. I can only contribute my brute strength to an adrenaline rush, pregnancy hormones, or spiritual guardians of some sort, but I was able to get him back onto his side of the car and regain control of the whole situation.

I wish I could tell you what the follow up events were, but I honestly don't remember. My therapist tells me I probably blacked it out as a way to protect myself, and at this point I want to thank my brain for doing that for me. I can't imagine after that part of the conversation it got any better. I do know, however, that I got him to his aunt's house and I cried all the way back home. I sang Taylor Swift's 'Teardrops on my Guitar' the whole drive back to my bed, as one dramatic pregnant teen does. The morning sickness started up when I was about a half hour from home, lucky for me I had a whole setup for when I had to throw up while driving, and I was really good at it.

I got back home that night and laid down. I couldn't fall asleep again because of the adrenaline still coursing through my veins from the events in the hours previous. I laid there making excuses for his behavior. He was drunk, he didn't mean it. We are going to have a kid together, he'll change, he's going to get it all out of his system by the time the baby is here.

Spoiler alert - he did not.

My son is 14, and my relationship with my ex is still about the same as it was since we walked away from each other that day in July. Non existent.

I don't know what experiences life has handed him. I don't know if he is still the same person as he once was. I don't know if he'll ever find the strength to change and heal whatever is wrong in his own mind, but my advice to him now is to make that priority number two. Next to putting down the alcohol. Not that anyone was asking.

Hindsight is better than 20/20. I looked at every detail and every scenario in whichever ways this could have gone.

I dont know why I ever even spoke to him again after that night. There were no texts or acknowledgements or thank yous for what I had done. But of course there wasn't. There never was. He walked in the house and passed out the first place he could get horizontal. I left. Things like this continued to be a theme throughout our relationship; a source of a lot of pain and trauma and it hurt me for a long time. It still hurts. I'm still crying writing this.

Holding on to this pain only hurts me, though. He didn't and doesn't care. I don't know if he's ever cared about anyone else in his entire life. Maybe he cared too much and got hurt, and this is how he responds now. I don't know. But I do know this is not healthy in any aspect.

Do you ever really 'let go' of something like this? Can you? It's a memory burned so distinctly into my brain that I don't know how to just 'be okay' with it. Maybe the lesson to be learned was to know what kind of behavior not to tolerate. I don't know.

All I know is I got out alive. I have an incredible son, who is an exact spitting image of me, physically and personality-wise. Down to his empathy & sense of humor. If I never had him, it's very possible I could be in a grave at this very moment. When I tell you my son saved my life, I mean it. He did it on several occasions over the next few years, and even saved me from myself at times.

I don't know how to really end this section as it's a very hard and heavy feeling to just end with a snazzy quote or something - so I leave this here and end it, just as it is now. Sometimes things aren't wrapped up neatly and packaged with a bow. They end messier than when they started, and that's just what it's like sometimes.

Do What Works

I have nothing but good things to say about therapy. My current therapist is incredible and she really makes me feel more sane than I've ever felt in my whole life. One day I was ranting to her about how finding time to myself is so unattainable for me at this phase in my life. I told her the only time I have to myself is when I'm in the bathroom. She asked me if I had ever considered bringing my journal into the bathroom with me. At first this sounded a little weird. I said, 'I never even thought of that... I guess I could do that and just write before or after I shower or just go in there and sit on the floor and journal."

She looked at me through that Google Duo screen and gave me a grin. "You just have to do what works for you, girl... who cares about what anyone else thinks about it."

This quote has stuck with me since the day she said it. Is journaling in the bathroom ideal? Not for me, no, not exactly - But in that moment, it worked. My self reflection time started becoming so important to me, that I started scheduling time out in my day to complete it. I looked for small times to write - when I was waiting for water to boil while making dinner or while the girls brushed their teeth before bed. Then I moved to waking up early just to write. I stopped doing all the mindless scrolling on social media and look! I made a whole ass book out of all my thoughts and feelings.

You don't have to do things perfectly. You can start any goal so small. I decided I wanted to start going to the gym for the sole purpose that I only sit at home and needed to get my body moving some more. I enjoy weight lifting and yoga, so figured I would alternate between the two activities. The first week my goal was only to be mindful of the week at the open times I had where I could potentially squeeze in some yoga at home or where I might be able to carve out some time to get to the gym to work out for a while. After about a week, I found that either right away in the morning (which would put me waking up at 4 AM) or directly after work would be best. I got off work pretty early in the afternoon, so I could get to the gym after lunch rush and before the after work crew came in.

The next week my goal was only to get to the gym three times. I didn't set an expectation that I had to go in or even work out. I just had to make it to the parking lot. I decided I could sit in the parking lot and listen to a podcast, I could go in if I wanted to... I could go for a walk and walk by it. As long as I got there three times that week was all that mattered. I just alter these goals tiny bit, by tiny bit. That's it. That's the process.

The cool thing about goals is that you get to make them. Your stipulations can be as lenient or stringent as you want them to be. You can make your steps little or big. For me, the smaller I start, the better. Quite honestly it works better that way, anyway. You don't have to set them to anyone else's standards, and you just in the end, do what works until you get there. This method works for goal setting in nearly all facets of life. Next thing you know, you'll be a goal crushing machine. I can't wait to hear what you accomplish!

Scars

They're kind of incredible aren't they? The way they form over where a wound once was, stronger than the skin around it, and never again the same as it once was. There's one I have on the top of my wrist from burning myself on my oven while taking out something I was baking. I have scars from jumping into puddles and falling down on my way to the bus stop in high school. I have scars from being sliced open to remove some dying internal organs due to Crohn's disease. There is a divot on my nose from nervous picking at my face, and then there are those scars that are less obvious.

I am an anxious person, always have been. An overthinker, an over-worker and recovering perfectionist. These habits were born of the emotional scars that I hunted and gathered from my time of searching for myself and trying to find the type of person who could actually love me. In this quest I accepted less than I deserved. I allowed people to disrespect me. I allowed people to talk to me in a tone that I no longer allow. I've put myself in situations that I really didn't want to be in, just in the name of being polite and never wanting to say no; an event I no longer choose to participate in.

Being human, I am not immune to the triggers of these memories in everyday life. Some days these feelings are prompted multiple times a day and other days not at all. The smell of a mechanic's garage or exhaust will always make me think of my dad. The smell of Aqua D'Gio makes me want to vomit, and the mixture of brewing coffee and fried bacon will always remind me of summers I spent in my grandmother's kitchen. Certain songs bring back memories of heartbreak that I was feeling at certain times in my life and there are other songs that I can't help but scream-sing to with tears in my eyes because I feel them so deeply.

One of my favorite songs is called "Hurts the Healing" by Drake White. The song talks about maybe through all this pain and hurting, is where the healing takes place. We need to experience the hurt, feel the pain from these repressed memories and emotions to actually heal the hurt. The healing occurs within the hurt. Until one day, the thoughts no longer bring with them the emotion that they once used to. This speaks to me on so many levels.

Listen... I am just as reluctant to heal traumas as the next person. You think you're strolling through life just fine with all your repressed feelings and perhaps unintentional toxic behaviors and microaggressions stemming from all of this subconscious hurt. We wouldn't know though, because we've blocked it out. It's tucked away, folded neatly down in our subconscious state. We task ourselves into oblivion or don't sit still long enough to face and work through the hurts of our youth or childhood because it's uncomfortable.

It is uncomfortable because you don't know how or where to start breaking these scenarios down. We are concerned more about how we will be viewed if this part of us comes to light. We don't think talking about things now will matter because 'that's in the past' and 'there's nothing we can do about it now.' It's a funny thing when you grow up and come realize that your parents are just fucked up people with a past, too.

Being a child of the 'late 1900's' (as my kids so lovingly refer to it) mental health care wasn't accessible for me. There was trauma in my mother's life, and my grandmother's life and the mental health care they needed wasn't up for grabs at that point either. These unhealthy coping mechanisms are compounded and passed down generation through generation and really at no fault of their own. It just happened from our families doing the best they could with the information they had at the time. Generational trauma can result in toxic feelings, thoughts, and behaviors. The only person that can fix it, is you. In a world where we have vast amounts of information - it's time to start the healing process. If we openly talked about our feelings and healed from our pasts the world would without a doubt be a better place. I strive to live long enough to see a society with my own eyes that has empathy for one another. A society that values the voices of all people from all sides, nooks, and crannies of those living within it.

Unhealthy coping mechanisms are passed down generationally. We've been conditioned to 'get up and stop crying, you'll be fine" and you know what, that's just what we did. We all settled for being 'fine.' We talked ourselves into being 'fine' when we weren't. I've witnessed my own shortcomings as a mother with my kids in situations such as these. With growth, it's once you realize you want more than fine is when you start reflecting back on things - feeling the hurt and begin the healing process. Just like the physical wound, starting this process is hard. The distance between where you are and where you want to be seems vast. Just like when you get a cut in your skin it feels impossible that it's just going to merge itself back together, but with persistent care, time, a little bit of caution, and grace the wound heals. Maybe you're down on your luck and your wound gets infected and gets worse before it gets better. Maybe it uncovers some other underlying issues. In the end, though the wound closes and although that spot may never be the same, the tough skin blends in. You're able to touch it without wincing. It's rough texture and color variation remind you at a glance that although that spot may never quite be the same as it once was, it can still be a fascinating part of your whole being. The tenderness becomes a gentle reminder that things can be incredibly vulnerable and yet display resilient strength at the same time.

You are no exception.

Reflections

The first time he got physical with me I went into an emotional shock and locked myself in the bathroom. I cried just like they did in the movies. You know the scene, staring at myself over the sink in the bathroom, watching the blood drip from my mouth leaving a bright red trail crawling down the curvature of the off white porcelain sink until the jagged blood trail vanished down the drain. My eyes moved upward, face remaining down as my eyes met in the mirror. I spit out the metal taste that was filling my mouth. I was 8 weeks pregnant at the time.

BANG, BANG, BANG, The door vibrated against the frame as his fist knocked against the surface. I jumped with each strike.

"Open the fucking door, Jess" his voice sounded muffled through the wood grain. I froze, saying nothing. A few agonizing seconds later, "Open the door…" this time, through his teeth.

Out of all the things I had come to know in my life, in that moment I knew the one thing I knew I was absolutely *not* going to do was open that god forsaken door. Looking around there was no window, so no way out either. My phone was in the bedroom, inaccessible to where I was at the time. The only way out <u>was through</u>.

"Leave me alone." The words breathlessly escaped from my throat. I turned the 'hot' knob on the old faucet, beginning to analyze the slice on my lip. I wanted to know how far back it went, how deep it was and to determine if there was a way I would be able to hide an injury such as this one. "It was an accident. Open the door so I can see." the tone of his voice didn't match his sentiment. After all, moments before he was the one who caused this injury, and now all of a sudden he wanted to help? "This was HARDLY an accident" I responded "you hit me in the mouth."

There was an unsympathetic pause, "I didn't realize you were standing so close, I thought you were further behind me."

"You're 27 years old, why the fuck are you hitting people anyway?" I cupped water in my hands, and rested my lip in the small puddle I had formed.

There was no response. Yet I knew, every time I spoke I only riled him up more.

"I will be out when I'm done."

Truth is, I said this but in my mind all I wanted him to do was go into the bedroom and pass out.

"LET ME HELP YOU." He said it in such a way that it felt more like a demand than a request. There was no care or urgency to actually help in his tone of voice. I didn't know what exactly was going to happen when I did finally have to open the door. I wasn't ready for time to tell me just yet.

My mouth finally stopped bleeding after what felt like an eternity. I stood over the bathroom sink looking at myself in the mirror. Eyes swollen from crying, throat dry from trying to catch my breath. I splashed some water on my face, carefully avoiding my torn lip.

All I could think is, what just happened? What am I doing? How did I get here? I put my hand on my tummy, as a nonverbal apology to my unborn baby.

Whenever things got physical I always tried to make my way to the bathroom. There was always an attempt to make a plan from in front of the sink, staring at myself in the mirror with eyes full of tears. These incidents typically happened on a whim, so I never had my phone on me. Just a mere decade and a half ago; the times before we all carried our phones around in our pockets 24/7.

When we were looking at apartments he thought it was so weird that I placed a heavy emphasis on what the bathroom looked like. Was there a window if I needed to get out? Was it comfortable enough to sit in for a while should I need a moment of solitude? Would blood stain the countertop? What color was the grout between the tiles on the floor? These thoughts were all very, very problematic. That's what you do when you're in survival mode and survival mode is all you've ever known. This relationship scarred me for life, nearly every relationship I was ever in has, really.

Once my baby boy was born it took about two weeks before we were gone. The defining moment for me was when I watched my baby asleep in his swing while I, in his direct line of sight (if he could see that far), was pinned up against the wall by my neck. I knew in that very moment, I was about to make one of the most dangerous choices of my life. As I stood affixed to the wall with his forearm in my windpipe all I could do was stare at my baby and think, "My son is not going to witness these things and think this is how you treat people, and that this is okay." My thoughts were drowning out the words he was actually spitting in my face. Once he let me go I collapsed onto the floor, trying to catch my breath. He walked over and sat on the couch. Finally, I was able to pick myself up off that blue apartment carpet, going through the motions of my daily routine. Washing dishes, cleaning the kitchen, changing diapers, and feeding the baby.

I wasn't allowed to sleep in the bedroom because he didn't like being woken up in the middle of the night by the baby, and I was a co-sleeper with all my kids. Jackson and I slept on the couch so he could rest undisturbed until it was time for him to go to work. When he awoke the next morning, he got ready, bitched that I was worthless because his lunch wasn't packed, and he left. I was still on maternity leave and hadn't had any plans to leave the house that day until the night before. I made several trips down those apartment stairs, newborn in tow, to the hand-me-down Black 2000 Oldsmobile Alero I was driving at the time. The car was packed, bursting at the seams full of diapers, baby clothes, a bouncy chair, and more blankets than I would probably ever need. I grabbed my important things because I had a feeling that once he knew we were gone, he'd destroy whatever of mine that was left behind. I may not have known him for a long time, but I knew him and his temper well enough from our year stint together.

I spent the rest of the day at my mom's mentally teetering on anxiety's edge. It was a weird feeling to unpack all your things from a room you packed up just a few short months ago. I tried to relieve my anxiety by focusing on my now almost non-existent commute to work and holding my baby. I knew that deep in my heart even though this was not at all what I wanted for us, this was right. This is where we needed to be. I made the most important promise I've made in my life to my son the night he was born, and that is a promise I intended to keep.

I started shaking when I saw that green blinking light indicating I had a text message around the time he got off work. I took a deep breath, my hand shaking around the little silver phone. I flipped it open.

"On my way home"

That's all I needed to see. I flipped my phone shut, and shoved it under my pillow. It was just a matter of time now, before he pulled into the parking lot of our apartment to see we were gone. It took about an hour of him commuting before the calls and the beratement messages started. I shut my phone off. I heard some commotion downstairs. He was calling the house phone. I guess we still had those in 2007.

We ended up having to change our phone numbers. There was a

"conversation" had between my step dad and at the time my now ex-ish boyfriend. All I know is, that mother fucker never stepped onto our front lawn again. That was the last day I ever had regular contact with him. It's a weird feeling when your world falls apart for the better, even when you can't see the 'better' at the time.

After all, I am a hell of a lot mouthier these days. Shit, nowadays I might even fight you. But there is still a little pang of heartbreak every time I look at myself above a bathroom mirror. The memories of me standing in bathrooms wondering what I am going to do is now a thing of the past. The ghost of that girl is still there though, and when I see her, I let her know that we made it. She is safe and she is stronger than she ever believed. But most of all - we love her more than she's ever imagined we would.

Kindling

"You're never going to find someone that will *actually* love you"

"No one is ever going to want some young kid with stretch marks and a baby, good luck finding someone else."

"You aren't going to amount to anything"

"If you keep eating like that, you're going to turn into a whale. No boy is ever going to want to take you on dates"

"I am going to ruin your life"

"I can't believe you thought I actually loved you, that's so funny."

"You're disgusting"

"Why is this apartment so messy? What are you doing just sitting around and eating bon bons all day?"

"You're going to raise a baby on your own? Hopefully you don't mess him up."

"How stupid are you/can you be?"

There are countless other quotes that have glued their way into the folds of my brain from this period of life. Some I am not willing to publish because I know my family is likely reading and I don't think I could do that to my mother. I'm already being really vulnerable here on a very public level, very past my comfort zone. I also find it difficult sometimes to look back and see that young girl version of me take a genuine belief in all of those hurtful words, and watch her apply them as though they were true.

I have lots of people who genuinely love me. Turns out, there are plenty of guys out there who love to take women who have kids and stretch marks (gasp!) on dates. If my kindling suppliers could only see how much I *do* amount to. In fact, I amount to more and more every day. As time passes, my worth only grows. I invest in myself and my passions and it's doing me literal wonders. I mean, I published a book so... I guess I also amount to being an author now. *updates resume*

The thing is, I used all these words that were supposed to keep me down, keep me small and believing I was nothing and turned them into kindling. The more shit that gets spoken, the hotter my fire burns. The stronger my passions get. My spirit lights up like lighting in the night sky, and my thunder claps are loud.

It took one little spark of bravery, and I used the extra words for kindling, I accomplished things I never thought possible and my fire was off to a cozy burn. The kind of fire that us midwesterners live for in the fall. I'm sure as I try more new things that it's only inevitable that I will pick up some extra kindling along the way. Right now life is cozy. I have my family, my dog, a roof over my head, food to eat, yoga pants and sweatshirts to wear. I have my ability to take in the world around me via my senses. I am free to create, I am free to feel and at the end of the night I get to lay my head down in a comfy bed with a cozy blanket and do it all again the next day.

We're going to keep this fire burning. Because like a good fire, someday this life will come to a gradual end. I want to make sure I can really enjoy my fire and share my warmth with others before it's time to return to the cosmos.

We are only as happy as we decide to be. Watch where your thoughts go and direct your energy only towards things that set your soul on fire, for there isn't as much time as we anticipate.

An Equal But Opposite Reaction

One of the first self care things I had ever done for myself was start a gratitude list. As I've said before, I started with a baby goal. Every night before I went to bed I had to list one thing I was grateful for. Not long after, I was able to add several incredible things at night that I was glad to have experienced that particular day. I took this practice a step further and started journaling about all the good that was happening, and I found out why these things struck something in me that particular day.

It's that same situation that arises when you talk about something, you notice it more out in the world. Baader-Meinhof phenomenon. We are often so quick to point out all the negative, that it ends up being all we see anymore. Just like we have a choice to look at the negative - we have a choice to look at the positive. However, in American culture we've been taught to only focus on what we lack because that's how our system is set up to run. Capitalism doesn't work as well if we all were to love ourselves and become happy with what we have in front of us. Our economy is set up to thrive on our insecurities.

However, you have the ability to reject this message that is being forced on to you. We can reject this way of thinking because it's not actually *our* way of thinking - we've been brainwashed into it. If we can stop and look at what we do have, we will start to notice these little shimmers of happiness that we've learned to glance over or minimize any positive reaction to in an effort to only focus on what's lacking.

This gratitude practice was my foot in the door to self reflection and learning to heal some past traumas so that I can create space and capacity to learn and grow as a person. This isn't always fun and it isn't always easy. But just as there are sad times, there are good times too. I am able to find times that I experienced the joy in such large increments that my stomach hurt and I had tears coming from my eyes. I have made amazing friendships with incredible people and I've learned how to better take care of myself. When you take care of yourself, your whole world shifts.

An equal but opposite reaction.

I could spend my time focusing on my lacking mindset and always be reaching for happiness, just to find it's not uncovered under each rung of the ladder we climb. Which is what most of us do. It's hard not to with all the media or ads shoved deep into our eye sockets at every turn. Or, I can do just the opposite and put just as much effort into finding the little things that make me smile during the day, or noticing opportunities to create a memory, capture a picture - that's the equal but opposite reaction. The difference lies within you, the choice to see the positive over the negative.

We are able to control our thoughts and not let our thoughts control us. Sounds crazy weird at first, I know. I was right there with you when I started. It felt awkward for a couple of days, but then it really does get easier.

I've spent more time having conversations and laughing with my kids. We dance in the kitchen and we sing songs as loud as we can. I have found my combination of things needed to have a bath that mimics the atmosphere of my dream spa. Joints included.

Gratitude has been a life changer for me. But like everyone else, I can be inconsistent and some days I don't search for joy at all and wonder why I am in such a foul mood. I am just here to share what has worked for me in hopes it'll help someone find themselves and what they love and who they are - and not having to do it by anyone's standards but their own. But also keep in mind that falling off sometimes will happen, so plan for it. Doesn't matter how many times you fall down, but how many times you get your ass back on your feet.

Prioritize You
(And I Mean It)

Once upon a time I lived a life where I literally never took care of myself. Sounds wild, but I would go through the daily motions of getting up, taking a shower, brushing my teeth, and all of those proper hygiene things. These were the things I needed to do, and I didn't really even view them as 'taking care of myself'. It was just part of the mindless routine I was in.

Being a mom at 19 felt impossible because it was. I had skydived out of being a teenager to being a whole ass adult with basically no room to make mistakes. Also, throw on top single momming the whole situation from the start… No wonder I have such colossal anxiety.

My fresh son and I woke up on our second day alone together. He ate, probably pooped and then naturally, he was sleeping again because he has always been an amazing sleeper. I'm taking sleeping through the night before the first week kinda kid.

I needed to take a shower. When you're fresh off the birthing table and your hormones and tears are seeping out of your new mom pores at every given moment - the very first thing you need to do is shower. I had a conversation with myself that I couldn't just leave him alone while I showered. I didn't want to call anyone to ask in fear of being judged for being a bad mom asking a stupid question. This was being a good mom, right? Yes, of course you don't just leave a two day old alone ever, right? I over-thought it for a while and came to the conclusion that I couldn't leave him alone.

Naturally, I then spent the whole morning trying to figure out how I could take a shower. Do I just lay him down to sleep in his crib? No, of course not, Jess because if god forbid something happened to him this whole story would come out about how this stupid mother left her four day old baby ALONE while she SHOWERED?! I could already imagine the outrage. This was not an option. Looking back as I write this, I realize I was now in survival mode for the two of us.

Okay so... do I shower with the baby? This could check off two personal bathing check boxes today... but his belly button can't get wet. Oh, and how was I supposed to wash my hair holding an infant? I could drop him... will he drown if he's in the shower? The water could be too hot for his flaky baby skin. I won't even have available hands to wash myself... Can I even stand that long after having a baby? Okay, this isn't going to work either.

Moving on to our next option. Maybe we just don't. We don't shower. We wait until someone else is home and then we shower. But I really want to shower right now. My boobs hurt and I'm sweating out all the epidural and whatever else bedside cocktails the doctors delivered through the needle in my arm. I needed to shower.

Okay so maybe I sit the baby in a chair and just leave the bathroom door open? I could hear him, I could see him, I could shower, and I would only be a few feet away if he needed anything. After having your first child and seeing yourself back in your normal 'at home' mirror after the dust has settled, you probably won't recognize yourself. I know I didn't. I took a moment to cringe at my new self, and then I got in the shower. Popping my head out every few minutes to make sure the baby was still breathing, and that he was indeed, okay. He slept the whole time. So, spoiler alert: I probably could have just left him in the crib.

This is the exact moment I can pinpoint when I stopped taking any interest at all in taking care of myself. To be quite honest, my self care routine was basically non-existent anyway because I thought just practicing proper hygiene was self care. I will add the caveat with all my years of wisdom I have acquired over my lifetime, hygiene can also be paired with self care to make a delectable, soul nourishing treat.

I have never been super great with spending a lot of money on skin care, luxurious oils or body exfoliants that smell like a pineapple cupcake off the coast of some tropical island. My (very small) budget went to baby lotion and you know what? It worked for the time being. I started learning about my self care routine with bath time. This was an easy choice because it's literally the only time I was (am) ever alone anyway. For my self care journey, the next step up from baby lotion was to add tea lights. This didn't happen until my late twenties. The stress of adding two more kids will do that to you though, and I look back at that version of myself, the one who used to wish for the things I had now - just give it time - you'll get there. The tea lights; You can get a hundred of those suckers for about $5, and you'll have enough to last you a while even if you throw them away or bump them into the water on your first use. I then progressed to aromatherapy candles in my thirties. Maybe I'll just progress to bathing surrounded by a ring of fire by my forties - we'll see what happens. I am open to any and all possibilities.

I combined my bathtime with reading instead of scrolling. Sometimes I put on my headphones and sing really loud. I bought a package of bath bombs for relatively cheap and have added that, and a homemade face oil and hot oil treatments I made with ingredients from my fridge and pantry to my routine. You just have to start somewhere, and like anything else, ask yourself, "how could I make this even more enjoyable?" and you can find an answer almost every time, and if you can't - then you're in a good place for the next hour or however long you want to participate in this luxe atmosphere.

I can never over indicate the importance of prioritizing yourself. It doesn't have to be anything big or extravagant every single time, or maybe it is. I will not limit you to the amount of caring for yourself that you need. You deserve to take care of yourself, to have dreams and to live outside whatever box you think you're supposed to fit in. You deserve to rest. Rest does not make you lazy. Rest is a requirement for life.

I've had terrible body image and self esteem since the first time someone made a comment about my body in third grade. It took me far too many years to realize you can't shame or belittle yourself into being a better version of who you are. So, if you are someone who treats yourself poorly, you can stop now, I did it for 15 years. Experiment is over, no need to continue if this is something you're used to doing. We work from straight love now.

My years worth of luxe baths once or twice a week opened my eyes to find other moments where I could find opportunities to take things up a notch. A place where this is impossible is social media. Self care step number one (which I found out second) is to work on limiting your intake of other people's lives and whatever ads big brother decides we need pummeled down our throats next. My sister had told me about 'putting her phone to bed' at a certain time of night, or 'giving it a nap' during the day. Whatever timeline works better for you. This gives you time to do human things. Take a fucking deep breath, go for a walk, stretch your muscles, read a book, smoke a joint in the tub... whatever you feel like doing where you can be fully present. Recentering back to yourself and doing something non-digital for your mind or taking extra care of your soul's vessel is key to prioritizing you.

Some days self care is easy. You strut around your house in your thrifted bathrobe, hot oil mask in your hair, freshly shaven legs, body lathered up in lotion, drinking a mimosa on the deck. Other days it's realizing you could be taking better care of yourself and noticing your negative emotions, feeling them, sitting with them, and finding out what you can learn from them.

Maybe sometimes sitting with your feelings and questioning why you feel the way you do will bring you back to a time when you knew all you really needed... was a shower.

LOVE

Wow, how confusing, am I right? If there is anything else in this world that can be more difficult to understand or interpret I am not interested at this time.

The evolution of my understanding of the word 'love' has been a wild ride. When I was younger I loved everything. I loved the posters of Justin Timberlake and JTT on the walls of my adolescent bedroom. I loved shutting all the lights off in my room except Christmas lights that stayed up year round and dancing to music on my *sweet* sound system. I loved staying up all night talking on the phone with people I loved. I loved rearranging my room to better suit my space, and I loved my own company.

I had boyfriends that I thought I loved. Up until that point I loved the best way I knew how. Then there came a day when I found out I was pregnant, and another whole round of evolution of love was born.

In May of 2007 I experienced one of the greatest versions of love one could ever experience, with the birth of my first child. Unconditional love. Then again in February 2011 when my understanding of love grew two fold with the birth of my baby girl, and finally, my heart grew three sizes in July of 2013. These are days that I experienced yet another level of love. Then there was the day I got to tuck all three of them into a couch cushion for their first 3-sibling-photo, the purest love I've ever felt was born. I still catch a glimpse of that love when all three of my kids are laughing and getting along. They tell each other they love each other when they leave the room, or sometimes I'll catch it while we're eating dinner and laughing as a family of 5. It's a wholeness type of love.

Then there is the love that was introduced to me by my husband. I was always blatantly honest about all the crazy in my life and the baggage of emotions that show up by me typically lashing out. I don't hold back my anxiety, or depression, or opinions, or details of every GI symptom I have, and he still loves me. This is important, because it's the first time I've felt like I ever received love without conditions from a 'romantic' partner. It was really weird at first, but it was a new petal on this knowledge love rose I have been blooming in my head.

It's important to realize though, love has two sides. There are the positive sides that we all are familiar with, the giddiness, the perma-grin, the feeling of being in the arms of those you love, the times when love brings a smile to your face. But because love exists, so does great pain. This is the side of love no one ever wants to publicize.

Why would they, though? It's messy; being vulnerable. Disclosing ourselves in our dark moments doesn't fit the aesthetic.

There is the dark side of love that leaves you feeling broken, battered, and bruised. This can happen on so many levels. There is a chest-shattering explosion left behind when you lose someone you love. There are tears that come from your soul when your loved ones or children are sick, hurt, or heartbroken. In those times when there's absolutely nothing you can do about it but sit and wait it out together. There's the side of love where you sit in your best friend's living room talking about your worst fears and the only thing left to do is hold each other until your shoulders are drenched in one another's tears.

To know great love is to understand great pain. You cannot have one without the other and you'll never convince an empath like me otherwise. While this darker side of love exists, I have found in the hard times it's easier to surrender to what is than try and resist it. Find the little glimpses of positivity and celebrate them.

One memory I will forever hold dear is when my uncle was in hospice care, my family and I sat in collective pain in his bedroom. We all found a spot to sit, some on the floor, some on chairs, a couple on the bed. We all talked and shared stories and memories. We all laughed, we all cried and although we were on the dark side of love overall we had an incredibly beautiful moment sharing in our sorrows of what was to come. Instead of trying to resist the inevitable, we were able to surrender to it and make the best out of the time we all had left before all of our lives would change forever.

The darker side of love leaves us feeling vulnerable because there's no way to brace for it. There's no way to prepare for this hurt and even when you think you're ready... more often than not you actually aren't. So listen, you have to decide who on your team is worth facing this world with. You have to find the people that you're willing to share your vulnerability with and hold you up when you don't feel like you have the strength to carry on.

But most importantly, while we're still able - celebrate the fuck out of the light side of love. You never know when it may be the last time.

Just For Now

I often daydream.

I daydream what it's like to experience the silence that I yearn for most days. I daydream about summertime in the depths of gray, Minnesota winters, about a life with no financial stress, a life where I can actually go to Paris and eat croissants for breakfast near the Eiffel Tower. I think about what a perfect day would look like and I create the best version of my dream that I can, for now.

I can order a latte. The kind with the fancy botanical art on it, served in a cup hot to the touch in a boutique coffee shop. I can indulge in french literature, pinterest all the beautiful photography that's been captured outside the town. This daydream can influence an art piece, which allows me to observe one beautiful point, and inspect it into incredible detail, until I can capture my own photo. However, for now I have a hand created photo of this daydream.

I can make french food, or eat french fries from McDonalds. After all, this is my daydream. I can purchase a bottle of champagne and watch a french film enjoying the bubbles before cozying up for the night to go to bed. This is the self care daydream version I can afford for now. I would lay my head down to sleep probably with a belly full of baguettes. It was a good day.

I daydream of a day at the spa. This typically results in a bath by candlelight after some fresh air, bathing in the hottest water I can stand.

The tub is filled with bubbles from my fanciest soap, and a himilayian salt and eucalyptus bath bomb. I have a beverage of choice and a good book. I have my headphones and a lofi playlist echoing in my ears. I have an incense burning, and I breathe deeply. This is where I needed to be, for now.

It's important to daydream. Take a moment to think of something you'd like to do that feels out of reach. Plan an entire day whether it be alone, or with a friend and do the best you can, for now, to chase your daydream.

Take care of yourself, and chase your dreams by whatever means necessary. Eventually, you'll get there.

Slow

Slow is something that I've always avoided. It would even anger me. "OMG what is taking so long?" is a line that was commonly used in my repertoire on a daily basis. I was living in survival mode for so long I was always reaching for the 'next' thing. Whether this was the next book I was going to read, the next task on my to do list, the next motion that needed rolling through for the day. I did this for YEARS. I would task myself into oblivion just to avoid what I needed most, which was to slow down.

Slowing down meant having time. Having time to think about things that I hadn't been thinking about due to my never ending task list. If I was being productive, that's good, right? In society we are always looking for the next best, the upgraded, the better-than-ever version of everything we love. We are fulfilling materialistic goals of having 'stuff'. We are conditioned to believe that the stuff we have, and the more expensive and new it is, the more we 'fit in' and the more we are able to showcase (typically on social media) our successes to people we haven't seen in 15 years just to get a blue thumbs up or, maybe even a red heart if you're inspirational about it.

It's been about two years now since I've started experiencing my slow. Like most things I do in life, I started experiencing my slow, very slowly. I had to do it this way because it was painful. It was painful to stop and think about me and my feelings and my thoughts on my experiences because it hurt. Every agonizing second of this slow always (and still to this day) started with resistance. Slow was not in my wheelhouse because there was always so much self sacrificing to do to prove my worthiness to my friends, my family, my kids, my job... How would people know how good I am or how successful I am if I am not actively working towards the next best thing?

Slow came into my life at the right time. I started with self discovery. At 30 years old, during one of my slow mornings I asked myself this question that changed my life. Who am I? I challenged myself to explain who I was, without connecting myself to another human being. I told myself to avoid the words, 'mom, wife, daughter" ect... Who am I *outside* of everyone else?

I couldn't answer this question. I had no idea. Who knew that despite being myself for 30 years, I didn't have the slightest clue as to who I was as a person. I was launched into adulthood while I was still a child. I never had that portion of life that a lot of others have. The timeframe between high school and true adulthood, like paying mortgages and meal planning. I never experienced being a young adult, living in a dorm, going to parties, traveling on spring break with my bestie or making new friends. I never got to explore on my own, find hobbies, or any of those things.

I sat there for hours, trying to connect with this girl I've spent my whole life with, and I don't even know who she is. She's been told what to be, how to think, what to look like. I think I just fell into that in the midst of all my daily duties. Production was who I was. Production was all I had offered the world up until this point. I was a stranger to my own identity. When making decisions I never made them for myself, I made them in the best interest of those around me, even taking into account the best interest of those hurting me to avoid a fight. I didn't have time in my day to fight. I had so much maintaining of the status quo that I had no energy to go against the grain.

Slowing down for me was easiest when writing. Slowing down was easiest when no one in the household was awake, because I could do nothing and I could do it slowly without interruption. I woke up early to find my slow, and in finding my slow, I began to find myself.

I am a domestic abuse survivor. This only came to my realization when I started writing. I wrote like mad about everything that has ever hurt me, about my reactions and started making sense of them. I am a strong woman because of my experiences.

Sometimes when I am not in my slow, I go back to disbelief of who I am because that's been comfortable for so long, and that's been my response for as long as I can remember. I've wired my brain to think this way - changing this thought pattern requires stillness and reflection. The former does not come without your slowness. You need to slow down to understand. Sometimes for me this looks like journaling, sometimes for me this means sitting in the glow of a cozy light and drinking a warm beverage just noticing my feelings. Sometimes it's painful and sometimes it's the last thing I want to do. One thing is for sure, though, I never regret it.

When you start engaging with your slow and quiet, you learn things about yourself. It's a hard place to start, and most (like me) don't even know how to learn about yourself. One way I was able to do this was by asking myself questions. I became a toddler to my own actions, constantly asking myself, 'why'?

Example:

I woke up one morning with a heavy feeling surrounding me. It was like a weighted blanket of sadness. I sat on the couch with my pen and paper and started in with my one line of questioning.

At this time in my life, I was not interested in physical affection. Nick would come home from work, hang up his keys and come find me to hug me. This particular day he came up behind me and wrapped his arms around my waist while I stood there stirring whatever I was cooking.

My immediate reaction was to be annoyed, did he HAVE to hug me right now?

All he wanted to do was come home from work and hold me. My impulse was to clam up and just stand there in total frozen silence until the human connection stopped. Why?

I don't want a hug right now. I am bothered by distraction when I am trying to zone in on the task at hand. Does he not see that I am busy?

Why?

I am trying to make dinner. Plus I haven't showered, and I have been in the same pajamas since yesterday morning.

Why?

Because I don't have any clothes that fit me and I just don't feel great about myself at this point in life. I don't take care of myself.

Why?

I don't have time. I am overweight. I am not the same person I was back when Nick and I met all those years ago. He was attracted to me when I was incredibly sick and the smallest I had ever been. Now I am a chubby mom of three and hugging me probably feels a lot softer than it did before. I don't want to be chubby, I don't want to draw attention to the fact that I am different than I was before. I don't want to pay attention to the fact that I have abandoned myself and have lived on autopilot, which got me to where I am today.

Why?

It brings attention to my body. I don't want attention on my body and hugs are just the physical embodiment of attention by another human being. I was told once that no one would ever genuinely love me because of my body and how it looks now that I've had children.

Now that I've sorted through all the chatter about this subject, we're getting down to the real nitty gritty. Was being in a bigger body really THAT serious? Do you know how many worse things there are than just simply occupying a bigger body? There are SO MANY worse things you can be. The only person who focuses on your body as critically is you. If people do (because let's be real, those types of people do exist) they forget about it mere moments after they've had their rude thought and then they're on their merry way to the next destructive thought. And you know what? That is not your problem. There are beauty ads and big box retailers who make their whole life profits solely off of people's insecurities. You don't have to participate. I prefer you don't, but ultimately the decision is up to you.

There are so many more meaningful things to spend your life focusing on than the softness you may or may not have acquired over time. The past you is a different person, made of different experiences and you won't ever be that person again. They are a fond memory of a person who once existed. Let's live in the now and focus on who we are now, and set goals to chase the passions we have for the future. Let's focus on what our bodies CAN do.

We can go on hikes, we can do yoga, we can birth children, we can hug and belly laugh. We can dance and sing and watch sunrises or look at the stars with our friends. We can chase storms and know love. That's just the short list of things we are capable of. Embrace the new version of you, and fall in love with the things you CAN do, for a new version of you is on the way. and lets enjoy the version of ourselves we have right now. Again, sometimes it's easier to surrender to what is, than to resist it. There's meaning in it all and the world needs the version of you that you are right now.

Pride

There are some moments in life that you just know you'll remember forever. For me, my moments are on two opposite spectrums - these memories are either moments of heightened joy or inconceivable grief. Then there are moments when your kid makes you ugly cry in a mall because you're just so dang proud.

Twas the night before my husband's birthday. My son had asked me if we could go to the mall because he had a gift in mind he wanted to get his dad. After dinner that night we put on our winter coats and trudged our way through the icy barren terrain that sometimes Minnesota is known to be.

We stopped at a couple stores and I let him look around. I would point things out and say, "what do you think of this?" and he'd say preteen things like, "that's cool, but I want to get him something else." This boy was on a mission for something special. He didn't even know what it was, but he knew he would when he saw it.

We entered a local sports store and after a little wandering, he found it. He saw that bobblehead in the case and knew immediately that's what he wanted to get his dad. The store employee opened the case for him and my son held the bobblehead in his hands. "This is the one" he said, after giving the head a proper bobble test. The bobble was acceptable. This was the gift.

We made our way to the checkout line, and the store clerk was rattling off some sports information I was not at all understanding, but acted interested anyway in an effort not to be rude. He announced the total and as I went to grab my card out of my wallet and my son put his hand on my arm. "I want to pay for it." My eyes instantly filled with tears as I looked at my son's sweet face. "Buddy, no. You don't have to do that." He looked at me, because I was so embarrassing "Mom... stop. I want to."

"Jackson" I said, "that's money for you to buy something you want. I can pay for this."

"You're right, mom, it's MY money and this is something I WANT to do. So can you just let me do it, please?"

The cashier at this point was just standing in silence, watching a mother and son contend over who was going to purchase this bobblehead. "Okay." I said. I could feel my face getting hot as I watched my little boy pull out his batman wallet to pay for a gift for his dad. He was 10 years old.

The sales guy continued to talk to Jackson as he packed up the bobblehead. I stood back pretending to browse when really I was doing everything I could from having my face explode tears and snot everywhere. Jackson thanked the young man, and we walked out of the store. We got about 20 steps away from the store and I asked Jackson if I could give him a hug. My voice quivered. He of course, accepted and I started bawling into his little shoulder.

"Oh my god mom, are you serious? I literally just bought something" Jackson responded, unmoved.

"I know but it's so meaningful and you didn't have to and you insisted and it just makes me really proud. I am so proud of you."

"Thanks mom… can you stop crying in the middle of the mall now?"

"Probably not, but we can go." He smiled at me and we made our way out to the frozen tundra parking lot. He kept mentioning how embarrassing it must be to cry in a mall because someone bought something. *Such a gemini.* I wasn't embarrassed - sure it might've looked really weird to a passerby, but a lot of things I do probably look strange to outsiders and that's okay. Jackson may not have understood why I had a confusing, prideful cry in a mall, but just maybe he'll understand someday.

Reflection

I have had an issue with self esteem and body image for about as long as I can remember. The issue really escalated once I was in 3rd grade.

Third grade. You read that right.

Throughout my entire adolescence I did the absolute most to make sure my body was hidden. I wore big sweatshirts year round. Even on the hot Minnesota summer days where it's so humid and the air is thick - similar to how it feels when you open the dishwasher mid cycle and you get that rush of hot steam coming at you. I DREADED going to the beach and when we had our swimming unit during PE in middle school I was teetering on the edge of death by anxiety about getting into a swimsuit in front of my peers.

"Why do you always wear such big sweatshirts?" I was fully taken aback by this comment because no one had ever drawn attention to my wardrobe in such a way that seemed accusatory. "Because I hate my body." I responded before I even had time to filter the thought. "Oh, okay" was the response I received.

That response was the most mixed signal of responses I had ever received. Was it, 'oh okay' because now you understood why I wore them, or, was it 'oh okay' because this person thought, yeah, that's probably a good idea with the body type you have. V UNCLEAR. SO ANXIOUS.

Fast forward to high school and I did wear hoodies more often than not, but I also was discovering that I could dress to be comfortable and sometimes that meant not wearing a sweatshirt. My wardrobe evolved to include tank tops and tees, even though I was still fully immersed in thought about whether or not people were making fun of me.

Fast forward again, I got really sick. I was dealing with a bowel obstruction and literal dying intestine in my gut, but I was skinny. To me, it was worth it. I felt semi okay with my appearance. Nevermind the throwing up, being incredibly sick every morning, the chunks of hair that would fall out in the shower, and how my nails would spit down the middle with moderate pressure. I would see old friends and they'd say, "oh my gosh you're so tiny!" This was the ultimate compliment for someone who worked to hide herself from the world in fear of being 'fat'. So yeah, I felt good about being skinny but I was also slowly dying from the inside out so, that was a *little bit* of a downside.

Truth be told that when I was at my smallest, I was also probably the most unhappy I had ever been. My life was a mess, I was a mess, and I was lost in every aspect of the word. I was vigilant about being 'pretty' and desirable because I just wanted to be loved and I truly believed that not a soul on this planet genuinely loved me at that point in life except for my son. I was waking up every morning throwing up and feeling as though I was having charlie horses down my whole digestive tract every time I ate something. It was miserable.

My thought pattern at that time was so flawed. I remember thinking, "well i'm skinny now so this is going to be as good as my life gets!" I could not have been more wrong. I can't tell you the amount of healing and self reflection that goes into analyzing that memory... I just know it's a-fucking-lot.

The death of skinny Jess was a very difficult transition for me. I ended up having emergency surgery and a 14 day hospital stay where the doctors removed about 2 feet of my small intestine, some of the large intestine and my appendix. I was in the hospital for a couple more days as I was told I wouldn't be able to leave until I had a bowel movement. Do you know what is the weirdest feeling? Being 23 years old and having to tell your family and friends that you're ready to go home but can't until you poop. I think the funniest part of that whole situation was the fact that when I finally got to tell people that I was going home, they cheered for me because I was able to shit. Honestly I needed that encouragement and acknowledgement for such a menial, routine situation.

Time continued to pass, as it does. I got pregnant again - which really changes you as a person and how your body reacts to things. I started gaining weight and was so panicky about it. Knowing what I know now I feel bad for this girl who was so caught up in appearances. I wasted so much time and thoughts and money on my outward appearance when I have SO MUCH more to offer than that. Is being fat really the worst thing you could possibly be? No, the answer is a resounding no. I guarantee you that YOU spend more time thinking about it than anyone else does. You're obsessing over what is a passive thought to others, if even a thought at all.

I find it funny when people say they want to 'get back to where they were'. My question to you is, why? Our humanness *should* evolve. We are going to age, we are going to go through some shit that changes us. We are going to drink too much and snack on charcuterie boards with our friends because that's what life is about. Learning, growing, connecting. That fresh-out-of-puberty smaller version of yourself is gone now. You were a whole different person then. Bye, they no longer exist.

You've grown beautifully whether it be through your education, career, parenthood, grief, trauma, body... you are different now. That version of you no longer exists - and is the whole point of life not to move forward and experience things? We can't move backwards. Give that version of you a mental kiss on the forehead, wave goodbye, and let them go. You were worthy then, and you are worthy now. You have friends and family that loved that version and still love this current version of who you are. This version of you is incredible, smart, strong, and most of all, loveable. Focus on the now. Sure, we're a little softer, rougher around the edges, and maybe we've started a skincare routine in the interest of self care or wrinkle prevention. But whatever, it doesn't matter.

Speaking of wrinkles, I remember as a kid my mom was in the bathroom getting ready to go out with some friends and she mentioned her 'crows feet'. You know, those wrinkles you get on the outward edge of your eyes when they squint - usually from laughing, crying, or just any regular human emotion. From that day forward, I loved seeing those wrinkles. I would see them when she would laugh or smile. She may have been self conscious of them, but I, to this day, find them magnificent on her. They appear most when she smiles, even to this very day 25 years later it's one of my favorite parts about her. Had she not pointed it out to me I would have never noticed, but I'm sure glad she did.

I guess what I am trying to say is, you don't owe the world an 'attractive' version of yourself. Being thin, pretty, or desirable by others is not the rent you pay to exist in this world. It is also not the rent you pay to have valid thoughts and opinions. It literally does nothing for you in the grand scheme of things.

Love who you are now, today, in this very moment because someday not too far from now, you'll be someone different. We cocoon, turn ourselves to sludge, and we emerge as something more beautiful with each passing spring, and it's time we realize it and become more present now. Am I bigger than I used to be? Yes, I am. I'm also smarter, funnier, and have built beautiful relationships with people that I've met along the way. I have three incredible children, a loving and devoted husband, and I am (mostly) in tune with my intuition and myself. I wouldn't trade what I have now just to go back to being a couple pants sizes smaller - because I would have to give up all I have now and that's not a sacrifice I'm willing to make. I love where I am right now. Mess and bigness of it all.

After all, we are all just complicated beings traveling through time and space on a giant, floating, spinning rock and that's pretty incredible in itself. A grey hair and smaller body are not going to change that fact.

COEXIST

My husband and I were in a frazzled state one night after dinner. The kids were loud and crazy and the dog needed to go outside. There was an immediate mess that strewn across the whole kitchen, you know the kind. The one that appears out of nowhere once dinner is over and everyone has gone back to their spaces. Nick and I were bickering about something, the memory of what escapes me. I stopped what I was doing and looked at him and said, "I'm sorry for being annoying," and reached out to give him a hug. He hugged me back and said, "it's okay."

Hit the brakes. Tire squeal... anxious thought: wait... he really thinks i'm annoying? Rude.

I waited a second and said, "You didn't deny that I was annoying," still tucked in his embrace.

"Because sometimes you are."

Anxious thought: HE'S SUPPOSED TO LOVE ME! How can you love someone who you think is annoying?"

But then he popped in this little gem, because I know he could sense my energy plummeting, reacting in an anxious way

"...but, your annoyingness does not deter me from loving you."

When he said this, it was like a lightning bolt of comfort came down from the sky, turned into a fluffy blanket and wrapped itself around my inner child - breaking some kind of insecurity shell I didn't even realize was there. I felt tears in my eyes as I wrapped that last part of what he said around me like a microfiber comforter.

There's something about being a domestic abuse survivor and hearing words that say, you react to things in some way that bother me, but I still love you. When you've been conditioned after being called every negative adjective and tying it to your worthiness of love (because that's what narcissists do) to hear that someone loves you when you're not at your best is incredibly comforting.

I very much used to be an either/or person. Either you think i'm annoying or you love me. Zero room for in between. I only thought in definite terms which, when you have anxiety is a wild ride. Also might I add, not at all effective in this scenario.

You can be annoying at times and still be loved. Adoration can exist in the grey space between the black and white.

You can make a 'bad' decision and still deserve love.
You can be irritating and adored at the same time.
You can be authentic, and still be worthy.

Those are your people. Your ride or dies. The ones that will have your back regardless of time of day or distance in between.

When you find those people, keep them close. Companionship, love and understanding are worth more than money can buy. You'll need your people to help you face this world. Because it truly can be cruel as fuck and having someone to cry with feels way less isolating.

Thanks for the Memories

I don't know how the mechanics of how other people's brains work, as I have only ever been in mine. However, upon doing some self reflection I have learned that sometimes I have trouble remembering that people don't think like I do, oftentimes. I have made witness to several online articles about how some people don't have an inner dialogue in their head constantly and let me tell you... I *clap* was *clap* FLOORED.

My inner voice basically influences every choice I make in very major ways. But now, you're going to come and rain on *my* parade, telling *me* people out here are just raw-dogging decisions with minimal thought or even... no real thought at all? But yet, I have the 'mental illness' because I think long and hard about all potential scenarios. I do not have any knowledge on how one would know how to live life in this fashion. It literally makes my mind speechless - which rarely ever happens. My mind is always going even when I am quiet.

I started consciously trying to not constantly think. That lasted a whopping 6 seconds. Then, I did some research on meditation and thought that would be a good place to start. Although hearing that it involved sitting still in the quiet, just being present and feel what it feels like to be alive for minutes at a time was really fucking intimidating.

Like most new experiences in my life, the first few times I tried meditating it did not go well. I could only sit still for one or two minutes at a time before I would open one eye just a sliver to look at the clock. I would start getting antsy and start thinking about how I should be doing something more productive with my time. I should be accomplishing things and not sitting here in the quiet doing a silly meditation where minutes feel like hours.

One day I was journaling and I had come to a realization that the things I typically don't 'want' or feel 'motivated' to do - I can (and will) find any excuse in the book to justify not doing the thing. Now that I am a bit older and more enlightened than I was (but not as enlightened as I will be) I realized that me doing things to take care of myself I have always justified myself out of doing. I would deem myself too tired, too overworked, too sad, having writer's block, shutting off my alarm or any other number of reasons to not do something. While these things were true, and potentially valid at the time - I had come to the realization that literally every task I put off were tasks where I was being of service to just myself. Anytime I had the opportunity to take care of myself, I excused my way out of it.

Why was taking care of me not worth my own time? Why was I of service to everyone else but when it came to me I was able to have my only solid boundary? For the longest time I had thoughts that my value was only as good as my output in terms solely of other people. Carving time out for myself would be even less than a back burner priority for literal years of my life. At the same time, by no coincidence, I was having trouble figuring out why I felt so alone and so drained. I couldn't understand myself and I had zero sense of self worth. I had no idea who I was, or what I even liked.

When I would talk about myself I would use societal pre canned responses. I hated myself for it every time, because deep down I knew I was something more than how I am related to other people. But alas, being honest was never the answer I went with. It was too... messy. At that point in life I couldn't even tell the truth to myself so how could I expect that I'd be able to spew such trash believably, to someone else?

I also find that my best performances in self care typically happen on days where I am exceptionally resistant to do whatever activity I had planned for myself. These were the days where I wrote the best chapters of my book, the days where I said, 'I really don't want to go for a walk" only to find once I was out there, three hours had passed since I bounced down the in-need-of-repair stairs and onto the pavement. I now know myself well enough, that I am able to gauge what I really need based on what activity I am resisting the most. Whether or not I am ready to admit this to myself (spoiler alert: I am not) this is indicative of my subconscious thoughts of not being 'not good enough' or 'deserving enough' of good things for myself. I look back at past versions of me to how I feel about things now and it really makes me sad for that past version of me. Enduring abuse - no matter how long the duration - can really cause you to react to things in interesting ways. Sometimes these reactions are compounded over years and are embedded into your thought DNA and you convince yourself it's 'normal'.

I have been working on my mental health for quite some time now and a lot of times revisiting the past results in me breaking my own heart. While these things are hard for me to process sometimes, I am grateful for the ability to do this type of reflection. I offer myself grace, and tell myself what I would say now to convince my past self that it does, truly, get better.

This became especially important to me when I realized that I have passed some unhealthy coping mechanisms to my own daughters. I may not be able to stop them from enduring pain - but I can do one better and teach my own daughters from my own experience. In a way it's like we're learning together. I have the opportunity and responsibility to make sure they know to put themselves first, have their own best interest at heart above anyone else's... I want them to know they are 100% complete without the addition of anyone else. Because, that's what I needed to hear. I am going to tell you now, what I wish I knew then:

You are worthy and valuable. If anyone tells you otherwise, it's time to cut that connection off immediately. This is toxic. Do not let anyone make you feel like you need to water yourself down because they can't handle you at 100 proof. That is not your problem. Your dreams are just as important as anyone else's. Find joy regularly. Be as grateful as possible, experience life first hand & don't ever be afraid to call people out on their bullshit, because most people are overflowing in it. Whatever you find yourself doing, do it with your whole heart, and know that momma always has your back. This world can be very, very scary but know that any of the bullshit you have to deal with - I will always be here should you need to call for backup.

You will make mistakes. You will have to apologize for things you've said and things you've done. Failure itself is not bad, it means you just found a way that doesn't work. Failure and mistakes are not a reflection of your worth, it's proof that you tried. And the best part? You can start with experience this time. Anything worth doing is worth doing well. Brush your teeth and don't waste your time finishing a book you don't love.

Epilogue & Thank Yous

You did it! You made it through my first book. I made it through my first book. What a cause to celebrate.

As I was editing this book, I found it really hard to not go through and redo different sections. It's not because I didn't think those sections were worthy the way they were, but because some of my viewpoints have evolved in the short time since writing this book. I chose to leave them in the way they were originally intended for the sole purpose of what this book is all about - growth.

I would not be able to grow without my incredible support team.

Nicholas - thank you for holding down the fort while I work on my goals. Thank you for supporting me on every wild idea and dream I've ever had, for loving me and the kids the way you do, and for being the man you didn't have to be. You're the worst.

Mom & Becky - I would not be who I am without either of you. I love you both immensely and when we get to laughing together it's one of the best feelings in the world.

Amanda - My A1. Thank you for never leaving me. Thank you for being everything I have ever needed in a friend. My life is so much richer with you in it. You are so thoughtful and I don't want to imagine life without you in it.

Angelica - My soul sister. You came into my life just at the perfect time. You are everything I never knew I was missing. I can't wait to see what else we get ourselves into. It's always an adventure that sometimes even ends in scars. Worth it.

Beau - You are the best encourager that has ever graced this planet. There is never a shortage of compliments on anything I do when you're around and I hope you know how much I appreciate that. Thank you for buying my first book before it was even done. You're the man.

Jackson, Jaida & Ellie - You already got your own chapter, so I am going to keep this one short. But thank you for being the best kids ever. Thank you for being as excited about my dreams as I am. You are the most incredible part of my life.

The entire cast and crew of The Office - Thank you for getting me through years of life, and providing content for me to be distracted with while I wrote this entire book.

To those of you who purchased my book - thank you. Thank you for supporting me in my quest to live out my dreams. Thank you for taking an interest in me and what I have to say.
 You can follow me on instagram at xo_JessK6 or visit my website at www.jessk6.com to see current offerings and services.

About the Author

Jess, a Virgo and recovering perfectionist lives near Minneapolis, MN with her family. She has a really fucking cute black lab named Libby who she enjoys taking on adventures through the woods. When she's not writing, she's probably supposed to be. She's an introvert, so you'll likely find her at home in sweats doing some watercolor paintings, creating courses for her website, scream-singing, rewashing the same load of laundry again, or asking her kids why they just can't listen the first time. Jess is a domestic abuse survivor, certified yoga teacher, a tarot card reader, a feeler of all feelings, colossal advocate for mental health, Crohn's warrior and strives to make every experience as luxe as you can get with champagne taste on a kool aid budget.

www.ingramcontent.com/pod-product-compliance
Lightning Source LLC
Chambersburg PA
CBHW021938160426
43195CB00011B/1141